First Train Out *of* Denver

Leo Jenkins

Blackside Publishing
Colorado Springs, CO 80918

Blackside Publishing

www.blacksidepublishing.com

Publisher's Note: This memoir is a work of creative nonfiction. The events are portrayed to the best of Leo Jenkins's memory. While all the stories in this book are true, the author tried to recreate events, locales and conversations from his recollections, though they are not written to represent word-for-word transcripts. Rather, the author retells them in a way to evoke the feeling and meaning of what was said, and in all instances, the essence of the dialogue is accurate. Some names and identifying details were changed to protect the privacy of individuals.

Ordering Information:

Quantity sales. Special discounts are available on quantity purchases by corporations, associations, and others. For details, contact the publisher at blacksidepublishing@gmail.com, subject line: Special Sales Department.

Orders by U.S. trade bookstores and wholesalers. Please contact blacksidepublishing@gmail.com

Printed in the United States of America

Last Train Out of Denver/Leo Jenkins

ISBN 13: 978-1-68355-000-6   ISBN 10: 1-68355-000-5

First Edition 14 13 12 11 10 / 10 9 8 7 6 5 4 3 2 1

Dedication

This book is dedicated to Mrs. Adams, my eighth grade English teacher, and first person to tell me I am a talented writer. To all of the educators who motivate, inspire and believe in the limitless possibilities of those in your care, thank you. You make the world an artfully amazing and awe-inspiring place to live.

"No words quite describe the feeling that washes over you as you're walking out the door, leaving behind all you know, and hitting the open road with your balls on your sleeve."
— Stephanie Skovlund

Table of Contents

Introduction

Acknowledgements

I want to take a few minutes to speak directly to you, the person reading my words. If you've already invested time reading my first two works, *Lest We Forget* and *On Assimilation,* thank you. While both of those books are helpful in understanding the following pages, *First Train Out of Denver* is a stand-alone work. While this book is, at face value, a travel-adventure piece, I challenge you to look deeper into the content's undercurrent. Beyond the frequent social philosophies, another story exists. I implore you to discover it.

I won't be loquacious here because, frankly, I am not a fan of long introductions. I will say that writing a book of any length is a pretty massive undertaking and is almost never accomplished by a single person. Sure my name is on the cover, but without the efforts of Scoti Domeij and Lauren Chapman the following would closer resemble a series of verbal doodles sketched on a cave wall. So there it is, I managed to combine an introduction and acknowledgment all into two paragraphs. Here is to intelligently breaking the rules of writing…it won't be the last time, I assure you.

CHAPTER ONE

Mile High Mission

"How vain it is to sit down to write when you have not stood up to live."
—Henry David Thoreau

My right knee sinks an inch into the soft sand under the weight of the burdensome pack upon my back. The straps torment my tired shoulders. My senses are awake. A particular, heightened vigilance rekindles in me. The moon provides perfect illumination for tonight's mission. Covering my sector, scanning from left to right for any possible threats, another Ranger behind me does the same. The two of us survey the shadows. The scent of something resembling smoldering sawdust hangs in the air. With the ferocity of a war drum, the percussion of my pounding heart sends shockwaves throughout my tense body. *If we get caught we're done for. This is being alive. This feeling, this edge of everything we breathe for.* The cool night air delicately lifts the sweat from my neck, sending a chill down my spine, knowing there's no promise of safety on second-hand wings.

It's just passed midnight and we're using an old boxcar for cover in a train yard as we wait for the right time to board an eastbound vessel. The cool breeze is a surprise for a June evening in Denver. The fresh coffee in my travel mug helps to stave off the cold. It also does well to sober me up. *Who gets drunk at a baby shower?* I think to myself, as I shake off the incoming nausea.

Handing the mug back to Marty, he gladly takes a sip. At nearly six-and-a-half feet tall, Marty is an imposing force, even while on a knee. The thick red beard covering his baby face, tries desperately to conceal his grinning anticipation. Marty, a soon-to-be, first-time father, makes his presence on this mission seemingly reckless.

Marty whispers over his shoulder to me, "It's time!"

Instinctively we transition from security mode into a direct action mentality. Operating under the cover of darkness in hostile environments isn't new for either of us. We know the risk as well as what's at stake.

Marty takes the lead and climbs between two train cars. I stay within an arm's distance of his pack. The margin for error here is nonexistent. Neither one of us has prior experience stowing away on a train; a fact easily recognizable by anyone watching the awkward nature in which we climb aboard the last car of a very long chain.

The walkway along the push car is so narrow that our packs drag against the side of the train on our left and the short rail on our right as we make our way to the door.

Marty clumsily fumbles with the door as we both stand gracelessly exposed in the ever-increasing beams of vibrant moonlight.

"We're in!" he finally exclaims. Our heaving breaths separate the seconds. We each look around to see if the clamor our brimming bags made alerted anyone to our location.

The minutes seem like hours waiting for the train to depart. After nearly half an hour sitting in a motionless silence, we let our guard down a little. If anyone spotted us boarding we'd be caught by now. The fatigue of too many late nights catches up to me now; too many nights searching for comfort at the bottom of a bottle. My eyelids become magnetic, drawing toward each other like an unstoppable force of nature. Just as they soothingly connect, the heavy metal train door swings open.

The backlit outline figure of a man appears from nowhere. Quite calmly he asks, "Can you turn on that light for me?"

Marty finds the switch and follows the man's request. The stranger leans over and grabs a clipboard hanging from the wall that escaped our notice in the blackout conditions. The ragged conductor signs a form, places the clipboard back in its place and says, "Have a good night guys," then closes the door behind him.

After the longest thirty seconds of silence in my adult life, Marty shatters our collective reticence, "Well, that was odd."

I can't help but think we're being set up somehow. The discussion begins if we should exit the train. We decide we should just stay put, if he wanted us off he would have told us to leave, right? He didn't even act surprised that we're here. We decide to just stay in place. Despite the excitement, the weight of exhaustion pulls me back down. It doesn't take long before my eyelids slam shut once more. Using an old tan jacket as a pillow I sprawl out on the floor of the push car and wait for the train to begin moving.

I fall into a deep sleep: The kind where it doesn't matter what position your body is in or how hard the surface is you're passed out on. Two hours of hard sleep later and the train hasn't budged. Marty is not finding any more comfort in his awkward position, propped against the back door. The door flings open. My slumber is disturbed without sympathy. The all-too-familiar authoritative voice of a law enforcement officer commands us off the train. He wields the brightest flashlight I've ever experienced, shocking my rods and cones into submission.

Marty piles out instantly. I choose to move slowly and deliberately. I know what this looks like and I'm not willing to get shot tonight. Collecting the now filthy tan jacket from the dirty floor, I lift my hands to show the officer I have no weapon, put on my jacket and hoist the large red backpack to my stiff shoulders. I follow Marty's lead, making three steps through the darkness and out of the cramped train door.

Sitting on a pile of stones like two overgrown teenagers out past curfew, the lecture from the officer about trespassing begins. I'm not paying attention, all I can think about is the last time I was arrested for trespassing and how expensive it was. *What am I even doing here?* I ask myself. A week ago I lived in an amazing beach house in Costa Rica, now I'm homeless, unemployed and about to be arrested for train hopping at midnight in Denver, Colorado. ❀

CHAPTER TWO

Breaking the Ice

"Once you make a decision, the universe conspires to make it happen."
—Ralph Waldo Emerson

Trudging through the tenebrous morning, two feet of sticky wet snow compresses under my feet. Hours before the sun makes its presence felt, I reach for the frozen handle of my Dodge Dakota parked on the street in front of my small house. My mind is post-op Novocain numb as I knock the obnoxious, freezing white substance from my shoes for the countless time. The ever-advancing army of unique snowflakes descending upon me seems to halt mid free fall. In a moment of suspended animation and brilliant clarity, a single thought dominates my cognition, changing my trajectory irrevocably.

I don't want to go to work today.

That's it. I don't know a single adult who hasn't had the same thought echo through their mind. For several years, I've owned and managed a modest gym in Colorado, a role I fell into by accident. My love of fitness and inability to take senseless orders following my time in the Army set the stage for my entrepreneurship.

I've worked hard building this life, brick by brick. It's my blood, my sweat, I've made mortar from the mix. Smearing the emotional sealant upon an otherwise porous foundation. Burning my soul to build a castle so grand. Misplaced stones yield a labyrinth in its stead, one I now find myself unintentionally at the center of. I've grown weary, exhausted from the tedium. A life maintained in a perpetual grey tint, shadowed by the walls of my own creation.

As the frozen air blasts through the vents and converts to a temperature capable of melting the frost on the windshield, I think back to a simple promise I made to a friend years before. I wasn't there when James was killed in Iraq. In the days and weeks afterward, I fell into an absolute abyss. In the wake of that tragedy I made a promise to my fallen friend, and to every one of my brothers who never came home from war: I will do everything in my power to honor their memories by living life to the fullest. Too many of the best and brightest of our generation were robbed the opportunity to choose how they'd spend their twenties and beyond. The best way to honor them is to fulfill my promise.

As the virgin snow melodically crunches under the tread of my all terrain tires, headlights illuminate the path, and the solution becomes evident. Unknowingly, I've waited for this moment all my life and more. Life is too short, too damn precious to spend miserable. Before arriving at the gym, less than three minutes later, my exit strategy takes form. I will throw caution and myself into the wind. The next few months become as transformative as any I have ever experienced in my three decades on earth.

We are taught there's a certain way to do things: Take out loans to go to school, get a job, pay your taxes, get married, buy a house, fill it with things you can't afford, have kids, raise the kids to go to school, continue working at the job that you no longer enjoy to pay off the schooling and possessions you didn't really need until you have saved enough to retire, so you can finally enjoy life. Now more than ever, this pattern sours my stomach. There's something backward about it. Why do we put off living life until tomorrow when it's looking us in the eye today? After all, time is our most finite resource. It is the only thing we can't reproduce. Yet we foolishly burn it, an ignorant defiance to mortality. When we see death, we beg for more time, not for more money or possessions or power. No, we plead for moments. Go ahead, make your retirement plans. Life doesn't give a shit about your plans; and I no longer give a shit about fitting into that ordained mold.

To be lasting, the change must be drastic. To find myself now, I have to lose myself. To purge the synthetic layers of discontent and the weight of possession, I decide to sell everything I own, minus what will fit in a single backpack. What I can't sell, I give away.

The first things to go are items from when I raced triathlon, some race wheels, old shoes and other gadgets. I haven't used any of it in a couple of years. Even though they've done nothing but collect dust for years, parting with them is tough. I made incredible memories on those wheels. I reminisce about all the miles they carried me, and the races I'd won on them. Maybe it's not the object I'm attached to at all, perhaps it's the experiences I cling to.

My snowboard gear is the next to go. After working at a few outdoor stores over the years, my house resembles an REI. Every piece of equipment carried me through a different adventure. These possessions, a road map of my life, define me as a person, or so I once thought. The more I release the easier the process becomes, selling high-end outdoor gear for pennies on the dollar. Four snowboards, three bikes, a house full of furniture and more Gore-Tex than an expedition of five needs to summit Everest, all goes. What doesn't sell quickly, I start to give away, until the contents of my life fits into the pack sitting in the corner of my now-empty bedroom.

Every day, parting ways with my possessions becomes easier. What remains difficult is attempting to explain to the people around me what I'm doing and why. I'm met with a barrage of doubt-filled resistance and brimming insecurities from several people. My actions don't fit their mold, and that creates discomfort. That discomfort manifests into mild mocking and belittlement. For years, I clung to the belief that many people depend on my presence, my leaving them results in an egregious abandonment. The truth is, people are resilient, and if they truly care for you they will support your decision, even if it creates a minor inconvenience for them. If they don't support it then they never actually cared about you to begin with, and their opinions should not factor into how you decide to live.

The process inadvertently teaches me an exceptionally valuable lesson. People who interject their petty wants into a life decision that's ultimately in your best interest, which does not concern them, who do not love you and will likely not show up when you need them are best off ignored, if not disregarded entirely.

Over a few glasses of whiskey, I work out a deal to sell my business to a friend named Todd, who I know will not just sustain, but improve the already successful gym. Todd is probably the smartest meathead I've ever met. Well into those brilliant years of life where his arms still fully stretch the sleeves of his shirt; the color of his neatly trimmed beard has given way to the distinguished white of an experienced man. He's that guy you know who everyone likes.

Twenty-four hours after being placed up for sale, I hand over the keys to my pickup truck. For the past year I lived with a close friend named Iassen. We served in the military together several years prior. Born in Bulgaria, Iassen immigrated to the United States at a young age and maintained his bilingual ability, a skill I envy. He moved out to Colorado from Florida with nothing but his cantankerous old dog, Dutch, and a pile of clothes. He becomes the joyous bulk beneficiary of all my household goods. A mutually beneficial exchange, as he isn't really the type to shop for plates, and I have no desire to haggle with some stranger at a yard sale over an item that costs a dollar. I hand over the house key to Iassen.

There's no sleep the evening before my flight. A thousand loose ends needing tied tangle into a giant chaotic knot. Bank, phone, insurance, and countless papers to sign; the process, a caffeine-fueled cyclone, moves too fast for emotion or even much thought to creep in. My sleepless night turns to day and the list still isn't complete. T-minus fifteen hours to departure. I want my last day in Denver to be spent leisurely strolling through the museums I was always too busy to visit. Instead, I sit in a familiar café finishing emails and consolidating finances. Despite my disdain for goodbyes, a few close friends persuade me into a final dinner before heading to the airport. After dinner, I hand over my final key—the last remaining physical connection to the business I nearly buried myself to build.

I know the members of the gym, my friends, are in good hands. From this point forward I no longer hear the jingle in my pocket that represents the responsibility which comes with a set of keys.

Like most people, I was in the habit of tapping my left and right-front pockets and back-right pocket every time I went anywhere. Wallet, check...keys, check...phone, check. Now here I am without two of the three. I no longer own a key, something I haven't claimed since I was six years old. Keys are an amazing symbol for responsibility. Find a person with more than a few keys and I'll show you a person burdened by obligation. No need to remember when to change the oil in the truck. No checking the mail. No waking up at 4:30 in the morning to open the doors for the first customers of the day. A small, yet significant, device in the grand scheme of things. A key is a light object made heavy with the responsibility it brings.

I'd be lying if I said there isn't a certain degree of terror and self-doubt in this moment. My good friend, and now former roommate, Iassen, offers to drive me to the airport. I can tell he's excited for me by the way he talks, fast and filled with enthusiasm for the future. A quick curbside hug and bidding good luck and Iassen's taillights fade into the darkness of the evening, leaving me to take the first steps of my solo journey of self discovery. Moving closer to the grey counter manned by the feigned smile of an exhausted airline attendant, I can't help but feel I'm stepping closer to the edge of a cliff.

The flickering florescent lights of Denver International Airport buzz overhead as I learn my first of many travel lessons: Entering Costa Rica on a one-way flight is not legal. I am completely unaware of something called "onward travel." Apparently travelers have to prove they will be leaving the country within ninety days of arriving. I canceled service to my phone earlier today forcing me to try to find WiFi in an effort to purchase another ticket out of Costa Rica. I haven't even made it to my gate and I'm already messing this up. Perhaps this is a bad idea. Is it possible I've made a colossal mistake?

The tides of life pull me toward departure. A long time ago I learned not to swim against life's current. The time is now or never. This chance won't come again. The last minute $800 expense for a return ticket I won't use kicks me in the gut, but nothing will keep me from boarding this plane. By the time I arrive at the terminal gate the plane is already boarding. I have three minutes to just sit still, plug my headphones in, and listen to one last song before handing the freshly printed boarding pass to another overworked airline employee.

The wheels jar and bounce and eventually find their way into the plane's underbelly. Unsteady at first. What a taken-for-granted mode of transport. A mesmerizing and God-like feat not long ago. A parody of an angel. There's no turning back now. Whether I've just made the biggest mistake or best decision of my life is yet to be seen. Either way, there is no changing it now. My eyes are heavy, but my mind is full. That restless chaotic mind begins to really think about the weight of the situation. It's all gone, all of those heavy earthly possessions that weighed me down, are now the concern of someone else. Whatever tomorrow brings is completely unknown. It's terrifying, and exhilarating, and liberating, all at once.

As the thoughts of uncertainty begin to slowly dissipate and my eyes begin to close for the first time in over thirty-six hours, the elderly man to my left asks my name.

"It's Leo."

"Going to Costa Rica for a bit?"

"Yeah, you could say that."

"Where are you staying?"

"I'm not sure yet. I figured I'd think about that after I land."

"You don't say? Do you speak Spanish?"

"Not really."

"How long will you be staying?"

"I'm not sure. I guess as long as I feel like it's the right place for me to be."

"Wow, that sounds like quite the adventure. My wife and I recently retired and we love going to Costa Rica for a few weeks. What do you do, Leo?"

"Well, I guess, I guess I'm retired, too."

The elderly man chuckles in disbelief. Despite the foot-long red beard covering my face, I don't look anywhere close to the age typical for a retiree. I'm eager to explain my situation with the couple occupying the seats next to me. The plane taking flight becomes a new chapter in my life and these are the first people who I get to share it with. From this point forward, the statement, "Where I lay my head is home," couldn't be more accurate. That being said, these two are now my new neighbors.

I tell the story about selling my possessions and my gym and my visceral desire to travel and meet new people. It's evident from their facial expressions that they, in large part, write off my story to youthful ignorance and reckless abandon. After all, it doesn't make sense to my retiree seatmates to sell a successful business in your early thirties to simply go be in the world.

The five-hour flight passes so quickly that I never get to sleep. This is the third consecutive night without sleep, yet the excitement of landing in a new place keeps me alert and energetic. What a drastic change in scenery from the snow-covered buildings from where I just departed to landing in a tropical paradise boasting an endless sea of lush green palm leaves.

The reality of the situation hits me like a two-ton truck when I step into the wall of heat and humidity lurking past the doors of San Jose International Airport. I'm overwhelmed by dozens of men who holler, "Taxi, you need taxi?"

Something hits me. I quickly realize I don't know anyone here. I just landed in a country where I don't speak the language and don't have a plan. Until this point, I'd spent all of my energy facilitating the selling of my property and getting away. I hadn't thought much about what I'd do immediately upon landing. Unlike past experiences arriving at an airport, no familiar face waits at the curb to pick me up.

I push past the crowd of cab drivers to nowhere in particular. I wander around the airport with the giant red backpack, searching for anything that resembles a path I can set out on. It never occurred to me before, but airports typically aren't designed with the idea of leaving by foot. ❖

CHAPTER THREE

Pura Vida

"The best way to find out if you can trust somebody is to trust them."
—Ernest Hemingway

Unsure of what to do, I take a short tactical pause and flop my pack on the curb. *Well, this is what you wanted. Complete and utter freedom to go wherever you desired. Now what are you going to do with it?* I've only been alone in the world for a few hours and I'm already talking to myself. After a few moments I decide there has to be a bus station nearby. The bus can take me to the beach. The idea of simply sleeping on the beach until I find a place to stay adds a layer of excitement to the situation.

Walking back to the sea of soliciting cabbies I see a couple of the guys from my flight. It seems evident they're on a short vacation looking to party. They rented a car and are finishing with the paperwork. Maybe I can get a lift with these guys. They must be headed toward the beach. Instead of striking up a conversation, I timidly execute a brief smile and head nod to acknowledge their presence and pass by. I'm not good at striking up a conversation with strangers on the street. It's not a lack of personality, it's more like some misguided sense of pride keeping me from asking someone for a ride.

Instead, I once again stand silently among the shouting taxi drivers. One man approaches me and in broken English asks, "What hotel are you staying at?"

"I'm not sure," I reply without making eye contact.

The man doesn't entirely understand so he asks again, "What hotel?"

"Yo. Necesito. Autobus. Station," I reply, in what can only be described as terrible broken Spanglish.

"Ohh, you go to bus?" the chubby, sweaty man enquiries.

"Yes, I want a bus to the beach, to Guanacaste."

"It go two a day. It go soon. I take you, vamos vamos!"

I learn the bus station is a twenty-minute taxi ride from the airport and busses only leave for the coast twice a day. Additionally, the bus takes nearly two-and-a-half times as long to arrive at its destination due to frequent stops and slow mountain roads.

I ask the cab driver, "How much will it cost to take your cab to the beach?" After about two minutes of bartering the fare drops from $300 to $150. During my early twenties, I acquired the skill of bartering in the crowded bazaars during three combat deployments to Afghanistan. Just to make sure I get the best of the deal, I toss in the caveat that the driver give me basic Spanish lessons during the three-hour drive, a condition he gladly accepts.

As the car makes a sharp U-turn toward the beach I hear my uncle repeating something from my childhood, "It only costs a nickel more to go first class." While the soothing sounds of Madonna playing in a rickety, early-90s Hyundai for over three hours probably isn't what my uncle Ron meant, it still feels good to not be on that chicken bus.

A few miles past the airport the car pulls to a stop at a roadside convenience store. I get out despite being leery to exit the vehicle, which contains all my earthly possessions. I keep a sharp eye on the little red car the entire time we're in the shop. I consider going to the bathroom but have the mental image of the heavyset driver in his ill-fitting pants speeding away with all my gear. He asks if I am hungry and points out that the back part of the store is actually a small coffee shop. With as clear of a view to the vehicle as possible, I sit down with hesitation, for a much needed meal.

The cab driver introduces the dish as "Gallo Pinto" or "Tipico." I learn this is what Costa Ricans consider their typical breakfast dish, consisting of a couple of eggs, scrambled or fried, with rice and beans and occasionally a fried plantain. The rice is seasoned with some magical ingredient that makes it taste as gourmet as those swanky places that charge four times what food is worth, despite the fact it's served on a Styrofoam plate. And the coffee…no contest, the coffee is easily ten times better than anything people pay six dollars for at Starbucks.

Not having yet figured out what the conversion rate is, I pay with the yellow Monopoly money and get back a blue and a red Monopoly money and even some cool-looking, pirate-type coins in return. Later I find out the world's best cup of coffee cost about seventy cents. With all the accelerating power that a twenty-two-year-old Sonata can muster we depart and cruise through the hills, zipping around busses and rocking out to music made the same year as the shitty little car.

I repeat *'Como se dice'* (How do you say…?), one of the only Spanish phrases I know, during the drive. I point at an object and ask, "Como se dice." Eager to learn, I ask the poor guy how to say everything and he's just as eager to teach. The food and the language of a nation are, to me, two of the largest contributing factors to cultural identity. I'm grateful to already be exposed to both.

Part of the allure of this journey is the notion of disconnecting from the obstreperous tones on the World Wide Web. That was, until I found out that there's WiFi in the cab. That's when the language lesson stops and Facebook once again steals an opportunity to inherit a worldly experience. As we approach the northwest corner of Costa Rica, the green trees lining the road in the middle of the country begin to change shades. The humid air turns dry and the landscape begins to look more like Texas than the tropical paradise where we ate breakfast.

We're only forty minutes to the destination but I can't hold it any more. I've attempted to ignore the mounting bladder pressure since leaving our roadside coffee shop.

"Alto at el baño, el baño por favor." Two years of high school Spanish, and that's all I can muster. Sad. What is left of the little red car's brakes screech to a stop at a gas station in the middle of nowhere. Now I'm left with a choice. Do I ask him to pop the trunk so I can grab my bag out and take it into the bathroom, or do I trust this stranger?

This man can easily drive away with everything I own if I step away from the car. I don't want to be rude and tell him to pop the trunk. Why does it matter even if I appear rude? I choose to trust him. I have to trust a person whom I've never met in a part of the world I've never visited. I rush to the bathroom on the backside of the dirty little building. I try to go as fast as I can but the stream reaches terminal velocity. The thought of a self-induced hernia enters my mind. Try explaining that to a doctor in Spanish. Over a liter exits my bladder in a matter of seconds, as I'm desperate to get back to the parking lot, fearing I just made a terrible mistake. Why would you leave everything you own in that cab?

Rushing out of the filthy bathroom, my heart drops like an elevator with a severed cable. "Where the fuck is the cab?"

It's that sinking feeling you get when you see red and blue flashing lights in your rearview, but so much worse. My mind screams at my body to move forward, but the situation produces a paralytic effect. What seems like a lifetime is really little more than a few panicked breaths. Out of the corner of my eye a familiar figure appears. That glorious, chubby, sweaty, brown-skinned man emerges from around the corner with some kind of ice cream sandwich.

He'd pulled around to the other side of the store to park and grab a treat. Slowly, the ability to produce movement returns to my lower extremities. Back in the cab, and once again sitting on the piece of duct tape holding the back seat together in what has instantly become the most beautiful car I've ever seen.

With my faith in humanity restored, we rumble closer to our small beach town destination. The town of Playas del Coco, located about sixty miles south of the Nicaraguan border has one thing none of the other towns do that appeals to me. Something familiar. Prior to leaving Colorado, I conducted a brief Internet search of gyms in Costa Rica. There's comfort in familiarity, I suppose.

Over a decade before, while attending the Special Operations Medical Course at Fort Bragg North Carolina, I was exposed to CrossFit. Simply put CrossFit is a training methodology that focuses on functional movements done over various time domains while maintaining a constantly varied approach. Ironically, my departure was initiated from not wanting to go into a CrossFit gym, and yet the first place I turn to on my first day of freedom is a CrossFit gym.

I am ready to be homeless. I am ready to give up all of the things I own. I am ready to venture beyond my comfort zone. Yet, for some reason, I am not ready to give up this part of my life. I've carried it with me in all the places I've been. This intense form of exercise was my outlet after missions in Iraq where I watched my friends get blown up by a suicide bomber. It was my physical release for all of the mental commotion that occupied my mind. It was as much a coping mechanism as alcohol was, and I just wasn't ready physically or emotionally to part with it.

The only gym of its kind in the entire country outside of the capital city of San Jose and only 800 meters from the beach, it seems like the best place to ask the driver to drop me off. The owner greets me immediately upon arrival. Juan, a lean muscular guy who gives off much more of the surfer vibe than that of a gym owner, steps forward to firmly shake my hand. His jet-black hair flows to his broad shoulders. He maintains a laid-back demeanor, a stark contrast to the macho attitude I'd come to experience with a lot of other gym owners.

I hand the driver his fare, thank him for the ride and tip him by American standards. This act makes his chubby red cheeks stretch as he nods thankfully before departing.

I explain my situation to Juan as best as possible while he shows me around his gym. After speaking with him for a few minutes, I learn an apartment nearby is available for rent. He seems so genuine and eager to help me.

"You want see apartment?" Juan asks.

"Right now?"

"Si! I show you!"

"Well, sure, I guess. Not like I have anything more pressing at the moment."

"Que?"

"Ohh, lo siento…Si, por favor."

I've already forgotten about the language barrier. I'm going to have to try harder to speak slowly and avoid slang terms. Although the three-hour language lesson in the cab is already paying off, there's clearly a long way to go before communication will be easy here.

We climb into Juan's pickup truck, toss the oversized red backpack in the back, and drive for less than a minute and a half before arriving at what looks like a small penitentiary. With a smile stretching from ear to ear, Juan proclaims, "Here!"

The razor wire sitting atop the paint-chipped, crumbling white walls does little to deter my enthusiasm. If anything, I appreciate how authentically "Central American" the residence is. Two steel gates lay between the street entrance and the front door to the apartment. The sliding glass door opens to a steep wooden staircase. As I move up the thirteen wooden steps, the ceiling begins to open up above me. I can see the hardwood floor of the main level and another wooden staircase leading to a loft space above. The marble countertops and brand new appliances are a noticeably abrupt contrast to the prison-like exterior. Juan shows me the bathroom and bedroom areas, as well as the two balcony patios, each equally as nice as the kitchen.

My thoughts quickly shift from, *How rustic* to *I'm not sure I can afford this.* After all, the place is less than a hundred meters from a beautiful beach and a two-minute walk from dozens of bars and restaurants. This place in San Diego would cost at least a couple thousand dollars a month. Even though I have some money coming in from the publishing of my first book and a little savings from the sale of everything I owned, my budget is still very limited.

"What you think?" asks Juan.

"Well, I think it's amazing!"

"I think, for you, $300 a month."

"What?"

"Is good?"

"You want to rent this place to me for $300 a month?"

"Yes. You come to the gym and train."

"Si! Si! Yo quiero. Gracias!"

In utter disbelief I am left with a key and allowed to settle in. Like any mature adult, the first course of action is to immediately run around like a nine year old in a new hotel room, jumping on the bed and opening every cabinet and drawer in the place to see if any other unseen treasures exist. The place is stocked! Fully equipped with plates, bowls, silverware, pots, pans, sheets, even cleaning supplies. *Where am I? This is incredible.*

I feel tired and stiff from the long flight-drive combo, but am completely invigorated from finding this place. Dumping my bag on the bedroom floor, I pull out my sneakers, change into board shorts and head straight for the gym. It's a four-minute jog, a perfect little warm up. I'm beside myself with how perfect this place is.

Every road leads to someplace new, someplace unexplored. With an infinite number of possibilities around every corner, I can go anywhere and do anything. I purged everything to be in this moment, to be free, yet I'm pulled to familiarity. For years I spent almost every day in a gym, and now I don't have to go, yet it's my first action; like a criminal violating his parole within hours of being released from prison.

Deep down I'm still not ready to part with that comfort. Even though I don't speak the language outside, in this place I feel completely at home with a barbell in my hands. The way I perceived those possessions defining me, a portion of myself intertwines with the ambiance of this place. The stale fragrance of sweat, the harmonious dissonance of clanking weights, and the collective suffering of all in attendance combine in an unparalleled therapeutic addiction.

Costa Rica translates directly to "Rich Coast." The national motto, "Pura Vida" means "pure life." Four words never more accurately summarized a country. The vast depth of its beauty are surpassed only by the easy-going attitude of the nation's inhabitants. I spend my first evening sipping an Imperial beer on a rope swing in a roofless bar under the watchful eyes of a billion brilliant stars.

Dozens of my fellow expats enjoy the sounds of a cover band. Something stands out to me, but I can't place it immediately. Something besides my location is different. I scan the tan faces of the other gringos in the establishment. They seem different somehow. Then it hits me, not a single one of those faces is illuminated by the cheap glow of a phone. They're all completely present and engaging in the moment, laughing and singing along to the music.

What a beautiful anomaly in a technologically obsessed era of human existence.

Over the next few weeks I make it my mission to explore every corner of the small town. I eat at every funky little roadside restaurant and stroll through each shop at a pace that can be observed as lackadaisical. For the first time in my adult life the pace slows to a tempo that affords the opportunity for reflection, resulting in more questions than answers.

I begin working on a new book about the transition from the military into civilian life. In the seven years since crossing the bridge from soldier to veteran, I've spent little time dissecting the consequences of all my actions. This introspection is ultimately the hard pull on the loose sweater thread of my mind. ✦

CHAPTER FOUR

A Little Chile
This Time of Year

"To be yourself in a world that is constantly trying to make you something else is the greatest accomplishment."—Ralph Waldo Emerson

Fitness has been so much a part of who I am for so many years it evolved into a defining point for me as a person. Over the years the once cathartic activity became obligatory. Being good at an activity for me meant competing. I'm not sure where that came from exactly, but competing became stitched into the fabric of my psyche. I didn't know how to remove those stitches. Anyone who has competed in sports understands that having your mind in the right place is paramount. My problem now, however, is I no longer identify myself as an athlete.

Despite my diminishing interest, I manage to place first in the Latin American region in the worldwide "open" portion of the CrossFit Games competition, which consists of five weeks of preliminary qualifying events. Out of roughly 5,000 men, the top fifty receive an invitation to compete in what can be considered a semifinal or "Regional" event in Santiago, Chile. The winner of this event is invited to the CrossFit Games in California, which boasts a prize purse in excess of a million dollars.

When it comes time to compete at the regional level I don't even want to go. The cost of traveling and competing is more than my cost of living in Costa Rica for three months. Having won the open, there's an expectation that I will win the regional. This results in people from all over the world publicly cursing me for attempting to steal the single qualifying spot to the world-level event. Those people make wild, unfounded assumptions that I traveled to the region to take "their" spot.

The thought of it plagues me for the weeks leading up to the regional event. I genuinely don't care about the Games.

I spend more of my time researching small surf towns throughout Central America that I want to visit than I spend training. I decide to turn down the invitation to compete and feel a great sense of relief. The following morning I receive a message from a friend in the U.S.: "How is your training going?"

"I'm not going."

"I know you, you'll regret that. And not for any other reason than you gave up an opportunity at a new life experience."

She's right. The result isn't what I desired anyway, it's the journey, it is the experience. What an egregious error it is to deny oneself the opportunities in life, which offer the greatest potential to stimulate personal growth. What capitulation it is to avoid a discomfort that will ultimately result in a better version of yourself.

The attention I receive, however, is not all negative. As a result of the exposure, a local Tico named Javier, one of the fittest athletes in Central America, extends an invitation to train in San Jose. He runs a gym he owns with his cousin, Roy. Upon arrival, Roy insists I stay at his home for the next few days while I'm in town. Roy and Javi treat me like a member of their family, taking me to their favorite restaurants and introducing me to their friends. Despite Roy's maniac driving style, which frightens me worse than any combat helo ride, I feel instantly comfortable with them. I'm humbled and graciously accept an invitation to be a guest coach while I'm in town.

The final week before heading to Chile, Javi comes down to Coco to train with me again. He's stronger than I am when it comes to heavy weights, but it seems I have more agility. Unlike myself, Javier has the epitome look of someone who spends most of their time in a gym. Over six feet tall, with modelesque looks and abs to match, he's the kind of guy you'd naturally hate if he wasn't such a genuinely good person. I convince him to stray away from his perfect diet and indulge in a burger, fries and a beer and he shares some of his awful tasting supplements with me, a real odd couple of fitness enthusiasts.

Two weeks later, I land in Santiago at just after three in the morning. I have a hotel reservation, but no way to get there. A quick search the week before showed a couple of twenty-four-hour rental car companies at the airport. My assumption is that I can easily rent a car as soon as I arrive. The terminal is desolate. In a groggy state, I find the two rental car counters near the exit. Thirty feet from the counter, a shady-looking gentleman in a black leather jacket steps in front of me.

"Hey, my friend, you need a car?"

"Yeah, I'm good bud. I'll get one from the guy behind the counter over there."

"I have good car. I rent to you. Good price. Best price."

I attempt to move past him as he pulls his cell phone from his pocket and flashes a stock picture of some generic white car.

"Yeah man, like I said, I will stick with the rental car company." He waits like a vulture hovering over a dying animal in the desert.

"I need to rent a car," I say to the short fat woman in the green vest behind the first counter.

"No cars."

"Excuse me? You don't have a single car? None?"

"No cars," she repeats unapologetically.

"Why are you here then?" Confused I sidestep to the other desk. I make the same inquiry to the short fat woman in the yellow vest behind the next counter.

"We have only SUV."

"Okay, what does that cost?"

"One fifty a day."

"Pesos?"

"No, in U.S. dollars. $150 dollars a day."

"Holy shit! Does that come with a driver and snacks?"

Out of the corner of my right eye I catch the random solicitor crack the same grin you get when you play chess and your opponent doesn't realize they just moved their queen into certain death.

"You are better off going with his car," said yellow vest, short fat lady.

"That guy?" I whisper, "You know that guy?"

"Yeah, he is okay."

Checkmate.

Turning to the greasy-haired lurker, I ask about his car for rent.

"$45 a day. The car is good."

Good and stolen, I think to myself.

Against my better judgment, I agree to the rental. As we step out of the airport the cold night air attacks my skin. I'm now in the largest most southern city on the continent of South America. We walk through the empty parking lot to what I'm pretty sure is a setup for an old school property acquisition. My pocketknife is buried in my backpack, so I reach deep in my pocket and pull out the sharp fountain pen I carry specifically for self-defense. Holding the makeshift weapon concealed in my dominant hand, I scan every shadow as we walk further into the night. The aura of attack is imminent. Parked by itself in a place that's clearly not a designated parking spot, I see the four-door white car and position myself in the least vulnerable position that I can.

The man pulls some generic rental papers from the inside of the car and places them on the warm hood as he searches for his pen. Glancing down he notices the fountain pen I hold more like a stabbing instrument than a writing tool.

"Oh, you have pen, okay my friend."

I blink in silence as the stressful weight of impending victimhood shifts from my shoulders to his. I see the brimming confidence deflate from his eyes as he recognizes he's in a dark airport parking lot with a very dangerous man. I have nothing to fear, for I am frightening. I hand him the pen. He begins a series of instructions in a now-cracking voice.

"I will need a credit card number in case anything happens. It's for the deposit."

I know he doesn't have any way to run my card. I spent my final day in Denver consolidating my accounts. In the process I cancelled two credit cards and closed down one checking account. However, I kept those cards in my wallet. I hand the man my cancelled MasterCard and watch him futilely write down the numbers and expiration date.

"You will need to pay cash before taking the car."

"How much?"

"The price is $500 U.S. dollars."

"Ha-ha, I don't carry five hundred dollars cash on me when I travel." I've rented a lot of cars in a lot of different countries, but I've never, not once, paid cash. This situation somehow becomes more dubious by the minute.

"Don't worry, there's a machine in the airport. We go to after."

I'm not keen on the idea of paying with cash, but I figure if I wreck the thing I'm not going to pay for it. The address he writes down from my license hasn't been updated in years.

To my surprise no one jumps out and attacks me in the parking lot. I pull out the money and pay cash for what I now, am almost certain of, is a stolen car. It is just after four in the morning and I kind of don't care. Before driving away, he instructs me to meet him back at this very spot on the morning I'm scheduled to fly out. That concludes one of the strangest transactions I've ever experienced.

I drive around the deserted city streets, admiring the various styles of graffiti, observing the motionless serene carcasses of the street dwellers, resting peacefully on their cardboard residences.

Not being able to check into my hotel until noon, the backseat of the car doubles as my bed until just after the sun peeks into the windows and convinces my tired eyes to open. I wash up in the bathroom of the small coffee shop I slept in front of.

Santiago quickly becomes the interesting experience I hoped for. I plan to take full advantage of having a vehicle to explore as much of the city as possible in the days before the competition begins. It takes over an hour to track down my first South American purchase, a wall outlet adapter. Javier and I arranged to stay together and split costs. It will be helpful having someone with me fluent in both English and Spanish, as very few people in this area speak my language. Since Javier arrives in Santiago tomorrow, I'm left to check into the hotel on my own.

This is my third consecutive year competing at this level, but it is Javier's first. Javi is the only other male from our country of Costa Rica to qualify for the event. I help him with preparations and he helps me with my Spanish. We joke that maybe he's better off not being seen in public with the gringo who's coming to steal the single Latino spot to the Games.

I take full advantage of the chance to speak Spanish with a person who's bilingual. I ask Javier to let me know if I mess something up when I speak so I can learn. When Javier arrives, we set out to buy lunch, and I ask in Spanish, "Where are we going?" He bursts into a deep belly laugh making me self-conscious about what I said. I really thought I got the words right, so I ask, "What? Was that wrong? I thought that was correct?"

"YOU... ha-ha-ha-ha-ha...YOU...." He can't stop laughing.

"What man? What did I say?"

"Ha-ha-ha you...you sound like a Mexican! Ha-ha-ha!"

I can't help but take part in his laughter. I never thought a Costa Rican would tell me I sound like a Mexican while driving through Chile. I have no idea I sound different than he does when I speak Spanish. Apparently, I adopted my accent from hearing the Mexican cooks scream at one another in the Phoenix restaurant where I worked when I was sixteen.

I'm learning firsthand that old habits die hard. One of my habits for the past three years has been to make pancakes once a week, typically on Friday mornings. A sort of cathartic ritual. Something about the process was soothing. Being in a hotel, however, makes this difficult so I'm forced to compromise and look for a brunch café. A fact I'm unaware of upon entering South America; brunch is as common as a snow leopard in Arizona. Even with a third degree black belt in Google, I can only find one place, on the other side of the city, which has a pancake breakfast. The lack of options makes the decision easy enough, finding the place will be a next level kind of mission though.

Despite not having the same love of flapjacks, Javier is willing to seek out the rare breakfast treat with me. The drive is just under an hour through the frantic city traffic. Unable to spot the location from the car, we opt to park in a large garage. The tires screech each time they turn deeper into the subterranean lot.

To our surprise the single elevator brings us up into the lobby of an exquisite hotel. Like a movie, men in funny little hats carry fancy bags with white-gloved hands. As we step to the giant brass door, a subtle, yet familiar, detail jumps out at me. Three men in dark suits stand at the door. A small, almost unnoticeable electronic device sits snug in each of the men's ears. A dead give-away declaring they're either FBI agents, way out of their jurisdiction, or a private security detail.

As Javier and I exit the building, a wall of sound slams into us. A chain link fence contains hundreds of screaming fifteen-year-old Chilean girls.

"I think they are here to see the fittest man in Latin America!" Javi laughs, teasing me about my placement in the open.

"No way, this is some Justin Bieber shit right here!"

Two more men guard the exterior of the building, hands clasped in front, making every attempt to appear professional. We awkwardly make our way through the sea of adolescents who should most certainly be in school. No gang of hormone-crazed teens will keep me from the sweet indulgence of those glorious freedom cakes.

Back and forth we patrol the street where the café is supposed to be. Each pass yields the same result. No trendy pancake diner. In our rhythmic sweep of the street we pass by the same Denny's a few times. Each time we walk by the front door Javier comments, "They have pancakes."

"The hell they do! They have heated flour covered in viscous liquid sugar!"

Standing in a cloud of frustration created by prolonged hunger, commonly referred to as hanger, we hear a group of fit people speaking in Spanish and looking in our direction. After a closer look I see that most of them are draped in different various CrossFit-labeled clothing. It's evident they're talking about us, as they're making every effort not to stare in our direction.

I nod toward them and give a, "Que paso!"in what I assume is a Mexican accent.

Excitedly, they all wave in unison. One of the ladies in the group leans to one of the guys and I overhear her say, "I told you it was him, that's Leonidas."

He says something in response, fast and unrecognizable to me. We all shake hands and as we begin to introduce ourselves, their party of six is called into Denny's. Typically, I'd invite myself into the group, but I can't do it. My heart is set on the lemon blueberry poppy seed pancakes advertised by the mysterious bistro that supposedly exists in this neighborhood. Parting ways, I ask Javier what the guy said in Spanish.

"He said, 'I thought he'd be a lot bigger.'"

"Ohh yeah? Well, he's gonna find out this weekend!" I joke as the search continue for what will now be lunch. As we walk I tell Javier the story about being in the military and traveling home to meet the families of the guys I served with and how every time I finally met someone's dad or girlfriend, the first thing out of their mouth was, "This is Leo? I thought he'd be bigger."

It takes another hour to find our target. The reward for our collective patience is well worth it. When Javier looks at the menu his eyes grow much larger than his empty stomach. We both over order copious amounts of lemon blueberry poppy seed pancakes, bacon, and eggs. As we sit, devouring the bounty of our mission, I can't help but notice the collective amalgamation of languages floating in the air. A half-dozen European nations all represented in this tiny place leads me to believe that brunch is popular in every nation, sans South America.

Later in the afternoon Javier and I check in for the event. Every athlete competing is here, along with the judges and a few of the fans. Entering the arena, it feels like I have a bull's-eye on my back. I think we're the last two competitors to arrive. Like Mowgli in *The Jungle Book,* I can feel the eyes of dozens of predators affixed to my every movement. The bushy red beard clearly gives away my identity as we push through the crowd.

"Hey! Leonidas!" I hear from one random person, and then another a few steps later.

I joke as we walk through the venue, "You might wanna keep your distance, Javier. You don't want to be seen with the gringo who's come to steal from Latin America."

Following the athlete check in and rule briefing, we're both eager to get off our feet and back to the hotel. As Javier and I make our way to the front door, a very attractive voluptuous Hispanic woman with a microphone grabs me.

"You didn't think you were going to get out of here without talking to me did you?" she says playfully, pointing to the cameraman a few feet away.

"I didn't think much of anything, other than I'm overdue for a sandwich and a beer."

"Well, you get to talk to me first."

A man with a shoulder-mounted camera invades my standard 'three-foot comfort bubble' and she begins asking me the questions I expect coming into the weekend. The focus of the short interview consists of inquiries regarding my recent relocation, all of which leading to, but never directly stating, that I moved to another country so I could easily qualify for the CrossFit Games. Despite having stated the reason for my move in multiple other interviews, people continue to believe what they want to.

Perception is an incredible thing. Perception is reality. The way a person chooses to perceive something is a result of their collective experiences and general outlook on life. Every experience, throughout every day, guides your current action. You and only you have access to that vault of experience. Yet, for some reason, those with the most limited access feel entitled to their opinions regarding my direction. It didn't really matter how I felt or that I repeated it until I was blue in the face, people who never met me, maintain a strong opinion about how I live my life. Beyond that, their opinions are incorrect and drip with antipathy toward me. One question in the interview stands out to me.

"Why did you move to Costa Rica?"

I choose to answer with my own question. "Have you ever been there?"

"Yes, it is beautiful."

She waits for me to expand on my answer, but I just stand there. That was why. It is beautiful and I needed more beauty in my life. A person shouldn't need more of a reason than that to move. ✸

CHAPTER FIVE

Sinners and Saints of Santiago

"Great things are not accomplished by those who yield to trends and fads and popular opinion."—Jack Kerouac

Three beers, two empanadas and a bag of gummy worms make up my pre-competition dinner. The next morning, I awake to a completely new sensation. It's my first time waking the morning of a big athletic event where I'm not at all nervous. I want the experience, not the podium. A relaxed attitude was not at all common for me. When I fought or raced triathlon or competed in CrossFit, I always seemed to miss the moment.

In the short walk from the car to the front door of the arena I'm stopped three times by complete strangers. Each inquires if they can take their picture with me. An odd request from my perspective, but one I am happy to oblige. This phenomenon continues throughout the weekend dozens of times. Even while I'm warming up, one of the event volunteers asks. I gladly set down the barbell, and embrace him in a big hug as though he's an old friend.

In an incredibly atypical fashion, I laugh and joke with the other athletes as we prepare to be the entertainment for the spectators in attendance. Normally my competitors were the enemy. I'd block out the noise of their voices with my giant blue headphones and cover my gaze with my hoodie on any other competition day. Now the experience, not the result, has become the focal point.

The first two events are held back to back, the first being a single lift and the other being a max distance handstand walk in three minutes. Each being very easy to judge. Immediately following the handstand walk, I look around and notice none of the athletes in my heat are close to me. I execute both of the events just like I practiced and the result shows. I place first overall in event two. Despite some of the resistance and negative emails I received before the event, I'm shocked by the response from some of the people in the crowd. A small section of spectators actually boo me.

In the hundreds of various sporting events I participated in over the years, this was entirely new to me. I've never been booed before. I'm here to have fun, to explore my physical capabilities and meet new people and I'm being booed? I display nothing close to poor sportsmanship, so why the hate? One would expect my first tendency would be toward anger or possibly resentment. It's interesting how much we allow people who don't even know us so much power over our emotions. My entire life I've never been good enough at anything to be hated for it.

The moment demands perspective. Perspective is paramount, and can only be achieved by changing my position. No, I'm not angry. The moment actually makes me feel accomplished in some odd way.

I head back to the athlete area. In route, the same beautiful tall Latina from the night before corners me with a big smile.

"You get to talk to me again," she says flirtatiously.

"So last night you were saying that you aren't here to win, but it looks like you just won that event."

"Ohh, I won?"

"I believe you did. Is that something you practice a lot?"

"I suppose. I practice in the grocery store, at work, in the street and pretty much any other place. I'm just a big kid. The world is a playground, I'm just here to play."

Despite the success of the first morning, I know what will come next. I'm the evil gringo here to steal the Latin American title. From a judging standpoint, the next event is not as objective. To say I'm judged differently than my fellow competitors is a massive understatement.

By the end of the day, I've fallen so far in the standing a podium finish is all but impossible. Videos from a few of my supporters in the audience surface of dozens of judgment calls made by the officials toward me that aren't even questionable, they're downright intentionally condemning.

Sitting in my hotel room later that evening, I receive a Skype call from my good friend, Marty.

"Hey buddy, great job today!"

"Ha, yeah thanks."

"How is Chile?"

"The empanadas are amazing!" Marty isn't surprised that the thing I'm the most excited about in a foreign country is the food.

"Hey buddy, I wanted to wait until you were done with this weekend, but what do you think about helping me with something?"

"Done!"

"You want to know what it is first? It involves a lot of traveling."

"Sure don't. I'm in."

"Ha-ha-ha okay, well then we leave from Denver in three weeks."

"Sounds good to me, I'll be there."

The rest of the weekend is more of a social event than competition for me. By the end of day two, I find out about the after party taking place the following evening. In the two years prior when I competed in the South West Region, there was no after party. During each of the events over the three-day competition, I try my best to slow down a little and enjoy the experience. The feeling of sweat mixing with chalk on my hands as I grip the bar, the clanking of plates and the rumble of the crowd become my focus. In years past, my thighs and shoulders were exhausted at the end of one of these rigorous events, now it's the muscles that stretch the smile across my face that are fatigued.

As I recover from one particularly miserable event, a gentleman about my size with an equally impressive red beard approaches me. I can tell by how he's dressed that he isn't one of the competing athletes. He introduces himself as "Adam." He's in charge of the equipment we're using all weekend. A raspy voice and subtle confidence accompany his well-trimmed red facial hair.

To my surprise he holds a copy of my book and a pen. "Would you mind signing this for me?" This immediately draws the attention of the majority of the people in the cold, cramped warm-up tent. I'd signed a few dozen copies before leaving Colorado, but never in all of my life could I imagine I'd be approached for an autograph while surrounded by shirtless Latinos, in deep South America.

"You wrote a book?" asks one of the other athletes, as I proudly sign Adam's copy.

"Umm, yeah. It was about when I was in the Army."

"You were in the military?" another asks. I'm still having trouble identifying myself as a writer at this point. It's almost as though I still haven't given myself permission to make the necessary internal transition. Somehow, the act of a relative stranger approaching me as far away from home as I can possibly be in the world and asking me to sign a book does something to ignite a spark of self belief and confidence in me. Other people take me seriously as an author, why shouldn't I?

As I struggle through more terrible, if not downright contemptuous, judging on the final event of the weekend, the crowd shifts. Perhaps they feel bad for me or maybe they witnessed my attitude throughout the weekend. The same crowd who booed me just a couple of days before now tears the roof off of the stadium with their cheers for me.

Despite my dismal placement, I achieve more than I ever hoped to. More people want to take a photo with me than at the beginning of the event than when I walked in, the favorite to win. Through my actions, I shift the collective public opinion of not just myself, but any future competitor who comes in from a different region. That growth is something you can't put on a trophy shelf.

The night out in Santiago following the last day of competition is the exclamation point at the end of a tumultuous weekend. An entire nightclub is rented out for the evening's shenanigans. Javier and I show up early and receive two free drink tickets, which disappear about as quickly as they're accepted. Soon the club is packed wall to wall with the fittest people in all of Latin America, dressed to the nines. My new friends eagerly introduce me to one of their finer traditions known as Pisco. Stepping through the crowd with a bourbon in one hand and a bottle of beer in the other, I hear another competitor yell my name.

"Hey! You want a Piscola?"

"I don't know what that is." You'd think I just told a group of movie buffs that I'd never seen *The Big Lebowski*. Shouts and jeers of disapproval permeate the group, drowning out the loud thump of the dance club speakers. Before I know it, I'm forced to relinquish my bourbon and I'm handed a brown concoction in a pint glass. Looking around I notice everyone else in the group clenches the same evil substance. Glasses clank in the center of our outstretched hands in the universal "Cheers" gesture. I take a hard pull out of the glass trying not to taste whatever South American moonshine is in the container. Looking around I notice everyone else's heads cocked back, finishing the content of their glasses in a single long chug.

"Oh shit! It's like a Jäger bomb!"

I try to catch up, but it's too late. Everyone finished their drinks and now laugh as I attempt to put mine back.

"Looks like you didn't win again!"

I have to laugh. Where I come from, teasing someone means you like them. Even though I know I can take everyone of them at this particular event, I welcome the jokes. I consider myself to be exceptionally lucky to have such a bonding experience with this group. Had I not boarded that plane from Denver a few short months ago, I never would have met any of them.

Several more Piscolas later, I see Adam. Bringing my book all the way to Chile for me to sign was such a moving gesture, the significance of which continued to impact me. I want to say "Thank you" and I'm not even entirely sure why. Even if I didn't know it yet, Adam inadvertently gives me permission to step away from how I'd viewed myself for so long; the person I tried to escape when I left Denver. I spent the past decade clinging to the physical pain of training for and competing in exceptionally strenuous sports. Those activities connected me to the agony of war, they kept it alive in me. They continuously brought me back to my warrior self, fighting for survival, depleted.

For a decade I carried, a now-withered, folded up paper bag in my wallet. The bag is just big enough to fit a can of beer into. I acquired it at a bar in Tampa, Florida, during Special Operations Medic School in 2004. It's nothing short of a miraculous feat the now see-through paper bag, survived for so long. I ask Adam if he remembers the part in my book where I write about the night I first obtained the bag. In perfect detail, he recites the story. I remove the wallet from my back pocket, and slowly produce the frayed keepsake from behind my credit cards. I hand it to my new friend, "I want you to have this," is all I say.

Adam is in disbelief that the bag is even still in existence and is amazed I'd be willing to part with it. He graciously accepts the gift and lets me know that if I am ever in Ohio, I will have a place to stay.

The remainder of the evening devolves into a series of blurred interactions involving activities, which I'm not sure are legal in this country, a post-midnight group McDonald's trip and a rapidly-facilitated room service request for an entire bottle of Jack Daniels at four o'clock in the morning. Thanks, Connor! ✵

CHAPTER SIX

Tamarindo Tide

"I hate to advocate drugs, alcohol, violence, or insanity to anyone, but they've always worked for me."—Hunter S. Thompson

Over the previous months, I became good friends with Juan and his wife. Since arriving, they've done so much for me. Once again, however, I find myself packing my single bag and preparing for goodbye. Before my departure, I want to enjoy the natural curling beauty created by the waves off of the Costa Rican shore. Juan happily agrees to spend his day off from the gym surfing with me at a beach forty-five minutes south of our small town.

Arriving at Playa Grande, we instantly see the conditions are terrible for surfing. In a sort of angry defiance the waves break wherever they damn well please. We give it our best try and even catch a few rogue waves that rise and fall without warning or regard for what we're trying to accomplish. Despite the dismal conditions, my heart is light and the smiles come easy. As we make our way back to Juan's truck I tell him that I will walk the forty minutes to Tamarindo instead of going back to Coco with him and his wife. He isn't surprised.

I think he knows I crave more of the ocean's embrace than what I experienced, given the amount of training I was doing. He insists he give me a ride.

The drive takes about twenty minutes on the washed out, curving roads. Tamarindo is a bustling little party town in the middle of an otherwise sleepy region of the country. Soaking wet, tanned bodies with surfboards tucked under arms leisurely stroll from ocean to open bar. The main strip features overpriced souvenir shops for sunburnt tourists, while locals pedal their homemade trinkets on the curb. I point to a little taco shop and ask Juan if he will drop me off.

"How long you stay?"

"No lo se. Tres, cuatro dias."

"I come back in three days, get you."

"Gracias, amigo!"

I pull my board from the back of his truck, slip on my flip-flops and wave goodbye as he drives off. It's an interesting sensation being dropped off in a town you've never been to with nothing but a pair of board shorts, flip-flops, an iPad, your wallet, and a surfboard.

The bartender at the taco stand greets me with the customary, "Hola, amigo."

After inhaling what are easily the best fish tacos I've ever consumed, I ask, "Is there a place to stay nearby?"

"Ahí!" he responds, pointing to the hostel sign to the right of the bar. He calls over the young blonde girl who works at the hostel desk, who I haven't even noticed until this point. She tells me there's availability. A shared room is ten U.S. dollars a night and a private room is thirty. I've never stayed in a hostel before and I'm excited about the idea of trying something new, but apprehensive about sharing a room with strangers.

As she shows me to my private room, I notice a group of travelers lounging in hammocks in the common area. After securing the only two possessions I have with me in the room, I walk across the street to the market. I purchase a small stick of deodorant, a toothbrush, some sunscreen, a bag of chips and a six-pack of Nicaraguan cerveza called Tona. Returning to the common area I start in on my dinner of Doritos and beer. The warm ocean breeze caresses my bare skin as the swaying of the hammock rocks me to sleep.

Just before sunrise, my internal alarm clock chimes, alerting me that it's time to flow to the ocean. Quietly, I grab my board from the room I paid to not sleep in and walk barefoot to the beach a few hundred meters away. The silence of the streets is vastly different than the boisterous party just a few hours before. There's a familiarity to the moment as I step onto the deserted, still cold, sandy beach in the translucent grey of the morning. I can't place it. *Had I been here before, in this moment? Have I lived this experience?*

Baptized by salt and sea crashing over and cleansing my soul, I paddle harder. Wave upon perfect wave pass through the ardor of my vitality. I paddle harder. Pulling water until the chaos lies behind me. In serenity I sit. That place where the ocean moves, but doesn't push. A moving mountain beneath my pounding heart still elevated from the journey past the break. Nothing between me and the epitome of nature in motion, but six feet of foam and polyurethane. With my back to the infinite ocean of unknown, I watch as the kaleidoscope of colors explode through the lush green leaves towering over the shoreline.

Bobbing like a cork alone, I realize I'd been here before. A different beach connected by the same ocean. It was years ago, but I'd lived this moment before. I traveled to this country with her. Some five or six years before we threw caution to the tornado and flew here. A madness that occupied us, or perhaps it was just me.

Perhaps when we sat floating together just beyond the breaking of familiar waves watching the sun crest through similar palm leaves it was just my heart that swelled to a state which stretched its very stitches.

That morning, years ago, floods my thoughts as the sun rises higher and one or two locals arrive on the beach. The thought of my memory heightens my awareness. *Was this why I was here?*

My previously clear mind is now a hurricane of debris and question. I return to the beach on the next wave in. One seemingly perfect expression of natural movement guides me back to the stable, stagnant earth. Sprinting, my bare feet burn as they slap like hunks of holiday meat on the sizzling grill of the now-scorching, late-morning asphalt.

I'm not the kind of writer who holds an obligatory number of words or pages to write each day. Quotas produce forced results. No, when the pen is warm and the ink is a river, the writer holds nothing higher in precedence. This morning, in that moment, my pen erupts, ablaze, with all the love and hate and remorse and jubilance of the world.

My skin isn't even dry when I begin to attack the keys. A heavyweight boxer doesn't strike that hard. Within the hour the leftover beers from last night's dinner sit empty on the natural wood table as I hunch over in the hostel common area. A quick trip back to the store. Another six-pack. Another bag of Doritos. The way the monsoons arrive in the desert of my youth, pouring without relent, the emotions of that period of my life pour into prose. I'd been writing my second book for months, but am unsure if I should mention her. I'm not sure if I have the strength to open those wounds and share them with the world. The contents of these green bottles floating up the memories and permeating my thoughts provide the proper motivation.

I write of Andria, the girl who agreed to go with me to Ireland before she knew me. I write of our relationship, the good and the bad. I write of the vitriol that stained us, and the resulting fallout. For hours and hours I write. I write until the beer disappears and my blurred eyes tire from squinting at the tiny screen. I still don't even have a shirt. I decide I need to step away. Perhaps there's more to say, but I'm tired now, and the entire day cannot be for reminiscing, some of it must be spent living.

I wander from shop to shop at no pace at all. I look for a suitable top, for the only articles of clothing I have are those tattered board shorts and flip-flops. As I reach for the metal handle of the tinted glass door of the fifth or sixth shop, a patron pushes the door open in front of me. She steps out, the familiar shape of her face, laughing, changes in an instant. Standing there, dead in her tracks, Andria.

She breaks the awkward silence, "Well, there's no avoiding this is there?"

"No, I guess there isn't. How are you?"

"Good, good. I. I, um. Oh man."

The last time I saw Andria was from the back of a police car. After we separated, she kept my dog. One early morning I awoke with the dog back in my bed and a knock on the door. I was arrested for burglary. After three days in jail and an expensive attorney, I was absolved of the three felony charges. She got to keep the dog I loved dearly for three years before we ever met.

The look on her face appears uncertain. I'm sure running into your ex-fiancé in a foreign country is always a bit odd, having not seen said person since having them arrested adds some awkwardness to that a little. I probably would have invited her to have a cup of coffee with me had I not just spent the last five hours, so ironically, tearing open the scars of our past. The interaction is quick.

"Did you follow me here?" she asks.

"No, I live here."

"Oh, right. I'm here teaching a yoga retreat."

"I figured."

"Okay, well."

We exchange forced stiff smiles and once again evaporate into the other's past. I laugh to myself about the notion I'd follow her to another country after years of avoiding her. I continue into the shop and settle on a light blue tank top before I return to the hostel with another six-pack of Tona. I sink my fingers back into the keys, quenching the fire with carbonation. A new article erupts from me, writing itself. I just sit there and watch the cursor travel seamlessly from left to right. In a single hour the beer is once again gone and I'm once again tired of writing.

With spectacular fortuitous timing, one of the girls staying at the hostel asks me in a French accent, "Would you like to go to the beach and do yoga?"

"Only if you promise to be gentle."

"I can't promise," she says flirtatiously in a slightly thicker accent than she spoke just seconds before.

"We're all going," she adds, as five more girls in their early twenties emerge from the large, shared dorm-style room.

Oh shit! I think to myself. *Is this what has been going on the entire time in the shared room?*

With the sun beginning to set, we make our way to the now hot sand of the nearby beach. Two of the girls from Canada have been traveling together for several weeks. The other three could easily be models. Their tall, slender figures and bright blonde hair tells of Scandinavian descent. Two are from Norway and the other from Denmark. Each traveled here on their own, but now they flock together. Safety in numbers I suppose. I never really give much thought to my own safety when I travel alone, but the experience must be incredibly different for a young woman. Situational comfort I take for granted must not come as easily for any of the members of this group.

Being a stocky, heavily tattooed, bearded man, I sense the women leading me to the experience assume I'm inexperienced with yoga. I allow them to continue that thought, not revealing the fact that I used to own a studio in Golden, Colorado and maintained a regular practice.

The same sun that peeked at me through those palm leaves a few hours ago now kisses the flickering ocean with a spectrum of vibrant orange. Taking our respective places we're led through a choppy Vinyasa flow. About fifteen minutes later, a local man strolls by selling burritos. I decline and joke, "I'd prefer a beer." Without hesitation, he pulls a cold can of Imperial from a shoulder-slung cooler. I can tell the transaction bothers the brunette French girl leading the impromptu class. As though I'm not taking it seriously enough.

Another few minutes pass before a tall local woman in a flowing ankle-length skirt stands over me with a Tupperware container. "Would you like to buy a cookie?"

Not really, I think to myself.

"They are pot cookies," she adds.

Well, well that changes things. "Cuántos?" I ask.

"Two dollars each."

"I will take seven please." I hand her fourteen dollars in colones and turn to the girls who've moved on to practicing handstands. I offer the cookies to the group, but am turned down. More for me. The first two go down easy with the help of what's left in the can of Imperial. Amused, I watch as each of the girls flop and tumble on the sand as they attempt to do handstands. *They're sober,* I think to myself, as I struggle to make out each of their figures through squinted eyes.

I kick up into a handstand and hold it for a little under a minute before the effects of the beers and cookies cause me to topple.

"How did you do that?" asks one of the girls.

"Do what?" I ask, as I pick up another cookie from my little pile, making half of it disappear in a single bite.

"First time I've ever done that, it must be these cookies."

"You are good at that! Can you teach us how?"

Until the sun collapses under the weight of the dark evening to come, I give my best handstand clinic to date. It's tough to tell if I'm drunk or high or just incredibly happy. The evening progresses and flows seamlessly from there. The girls insist on repaying me with a drink for showing them how to walk on their hands.

Serenity turned tumult, turned chemical tranquility turned blur of neon light and flesh, all in a single day. If the sensation of life could be bottled and sold in pill form it would no doubt be banned for its potency. Nothing synthetic can mimic the pure, unadulterated, overwhelming agony that is the jubilance of being alive and with an open heart.

The return to my condo in Coco Beach feels bittersweet. With only a few hours between now and departure, it feels like retreat and progress at the same time. The barren refrigerator reminds me that I'll be dining out again this evening. One more table for one in paradise. I order my usual, a double Flor de Cana on the rocks and Imperial. The sweet indulgent amalgamation of beer and rum jump-starts my evening. The only fit blonde in town, the one I saw strolling by a dozen times, once again catches my eye.

One of the English-speaking employees asks, "Do you want a margarita?"

Without thinking, and in my traditionally blunt and uninhibited way, I blurt out, "Do I look like a motherfucker who drinks margaritas?"

My cross tone smashes into his delicate sensibility. His face is shocked and apologetic as mine cracks into a Cheshire Cat grin, "I'm joking with you, I'll have another double rum, buddy."

Relief washes away his concern as he turns toward the bar laughing. Another meal of white rice, black beans and chicken. Halfway through my dinner, I notice a pair of brilliant blue eyes affixed to me and moving with purpose in my direction. I saw her so many times in this small town, that fit young blonde, without once having the intestinal fortitude to introduce myself. In a slightly cocky delivery, her elbow lands on the edge of my one-person table. With the confidence of a seasoned bullfighter, her lips part and utter an invitation, "You wanna get a margarita or something?"

All of a sudden a margarita sounds like the most satisfying concoction ever poured. My eyes expand and ignite in the cool air of the early evening. Over her shoulder I see the establishment's matrade begin to crack. Bringing focus back to those swirling blue pearls, I see mischief burning like a Roman candle. There's only one response I can deliver in this moment, this crossroad where desire meets temptation, "Do I look like a motherfucker who drinks margaritas?"

Unprepared for such a jagged retort, her pearls, those magnanimous swirling blue pearls double in size. It's plain for me to see she was put up to the joke. She, however, was unprepared for the punch line. I'm not sure how, but I convince her to sit with me while her friends finish their meals. I'm not sure why she's interested. I'm not sure what's in it for her, but she's affixed to me in a sort of predetermined way. The rest of the evening evolves into the single best experience during my time in Costa Rica.

Johnny Walker Blue Label Scotch, Trits ice cream, shotguns, curbside conversations, salty ocean air and an immediate uninhibited dive into the deepest crevice etched in the bones of our darkest skeletons make our first and last night together feel like some sort of foreshadow. A cruel joke, really.

I count the ticks of the clock between now and my inevitable departure, yet this person sticks to me. Why? The subtleties of her Canadian accent intrigues me as her blonde curls bounce effortlessly, flowing weightless in the night air.

Darkness, as it does, gives way to dawn. The clock, that cruel precise bastard, marks the frantic moments of our existence. That clock, that wretched twisting clock, screams it's time for me to exit paradise and return to my cold pile of remorse and heartache.

The cab honks. The single bag is packed. Her eyes say it silently, *Don't go.*

"Can I give you a lift home?" I ask, knowing her house is a half-an-hour walk away. She silently accepts with a smile. Like children, we hold hands rumbling down the uneven dirt road. The cab slowly rolls to a dusty halt and we each exit from our respective sides.

As if arriving specifically for this very moment, the sun sneaks through a partition in the dense palm leaves to illuminate one of the most unique moments I've ever experienced. An embrace like none I've known before. Timid, yet unafraid, the fingers of my right hand lightly slide through those perfect blonde curls and we meet in a truly superlative moment. Both of us knowing. This first kiss, this last kiss, both of us knowing. �֎

CHAPTER SEVEN

A Not So Triumphant Return

"You begin saving the world by saving one man at a time; all else is grandiose romanticism or politics."—Charles Bukowski

The menacing piles of snow I left behind several months earlier have since dissipated into the Colorado soil. Like the climate, the nature of my relationships also changed in my absence. People grow, they move on when you leave them behind. In all reality, I wasn't returning to anything. My home still hung heavy on my back, testing the durability of the double-stitched shoulder straps of my pack. My good friend and fellow Ranger, Kyle Fabra, agrees to let me stay in his guest bedroom while I'm back in Denver.

Kyle's home is a welcome contrast to the silence of my beach dwelling in Costa Rica. His two energetic young children set the tone of each day not long after the sun shatters my bedroom window. A part of me envies how complete Kyle's life is. Somehow he makes owning a chain of sandwich shops and caring for his family seems easy. Every day coming home from work to a house full of people that truly love him.

Marty quickly brings me up to speed on his plans. It seems simple enough. The two of us will travel as far as we can in three weeks with nothing but a hundred dollars and a backpack. People will have the opportunity to donate per mile. The further we travel, the more money we'll make for a charity called "GallantFew." We decide to leave in a week, at midnight, on June 8th. To my surprise, in the days following the announcement, many people want to make flat rate donations rather than by the mile. Marty and I incentivize people to donate large sums by offering rewards. I decide to up the ante a bit and put on the website that if any person or company donates $5,000 to the charity I will tattoo their logo on my body the size of my palm.

I spend the next few days promoting the event, tying up loose ends and playing with Jack and Lucy, Kyle's adorable little blonde terrorists. True to my procrastinating tendencies, I'm still not packed on the day we're set to leave. I burn the candle at both ends, catching up with friends and drinking quantities that would make a rugby team sick.

By early afternoon I find myself at a baby shower, of all things. I'm two steps into my friend's home, when I hear the host shout, "Leo! There's a bar. Big bottle of Jameson there just for you!" That isn't what I want to hear at all. I still need to pack. When I start tipping that green bottle, my grown-up meter plummets. A perfect sunny afternoon with friends is more of a beer occasion anyway. Until, of course, your ex-girlfriend walks in with her new boyfriend. Neither of us are amused by the other's presence.

"Hey, Matt…where's that Jameson you were talking about?"

I lose track after the seventh glass.

Marty and his wife, Lauren, arrive somewhere around my fifth drink. Since receiving the initial invitation from Marty to go on the trip, I maintained the belief that it was at the beseech of Lauren. There's solace for her to have a responsible adult looking out for her husband. Instead, he asked me. I notice the concern in her eyes mount as I open the next bottle of beer with my teeth. As the sun sets, we say our goodbyes and head to another friend's annual barbeque.

Of course, my reckless and fervent consumption only increases at this point. Like the company of a woman, there's something simultaneously comforting and provoking in the sting a shot of whiskey brings. The challenge of standing on weakened knees seems to be a byproduct of each as well. Perhaps, this is the root of my affinity for each. Perhaps that's why I pursue both with such excess. Hesitantly, my good friend Spencer agrees to trade shirts with me after my fourth slurred comment regarding how much more I like his than the one I'm wearing.

An hour before Marty and I are set to leave, our small group returns to Kyle's house. By this point I can hardly stand and still haven't packed my bag. Sifting through my disorganized pile of crap, I find a bottle of Pisco I brought back from Chile. Like a child finding their Christmas present a week early, I excitedly run into the dining room brandishing the South American booze.

"What in the fuck is that?" Iassen asks in a concerned tone.

"Ohh no, no Leo, you shouldn't have anymore to drink!" Marty adds.

"This…this is Easter Sunday and Halloween all rolled up in one!" I proclaim, as though I'm being pithy.

The hint of concern on Lauren's face shifts to full-fledged mortification as I pour the contents of the small bottle into a tall glass, splash a couple of ounces of soda on top and transfer the concoction to my stomach.

"Oh, Jesus. Leo is going to die! Marty, you're gonna have to carry him!" Kyle comments, as I return to the guest bedroom and begin packing.

My heavily-bearded, Viking friend and fellow Ranger, Austin, attempts to help, but exerts more energy laughing at my condition than assisting me with packing.

"What the fuck is this, Leo? You're about to go on a three-week hike and you have more condoms than socks!"

"Well, we can't have him getting Marty pregnant during their trip," chimes Kyle in his typical dry, sarcastic tone. The space between my ribs hurts from laughing at my own disaster. Marty starts recording footage of our soon-to-begin journey. Nearly unaware that all I'm wearing is a tiny pair of black silk Ranger panties and a white Felix the Cat shirt that's clearly at least a size too small for my frame, I'm urged by my friends that pants may be a wiser choice for the trip ahead.

By 12:01 a.m. our trip officially starts and I'm officially lying on Kyle's kitchen floor eating a gallon of chocolate chip cookie dough straight out of the container. My bag weighs 80 pounds. Through the jokes about my condition, each of my friends tries to talk me into leaving some of my belongings at Kyle's, but I'm not having it. My logic button has long since failed. A collective decision is made that I should eat before attempting to start this trip. Kyle calls one of his sandwich shops and tells them we're coming and to give us what we need. As we leave Kyle's home he hands me a travel mug filled with some of the coffee I brought back from Costa Rica for him.

"You're gonna need this, buddy. Ha-ha, good luck!"

We sit at Fat Jack's Supersubs for nearly forty minutes waiting to hear from a close friend who has inside information on our ride out of town. Our plan is to get a ride to the train yard just outside of downtown Denver and stow away on an eastbound train. Our friend, an engineer, has a tentative schedule of when trains depart and where they're headed. Unlike commuter trains, the schedule for cargo and coal trains are not specific. When the train is loaded the crew is called. Once that happens, it can be anywhere from an hour to three hours before the train leaves the yard.

Like Marty and I had both done countless times as Army Rangers, we sit patiently staging, waiting for the mission to be called a go. The conditions this time, however, are far removed and improved from the tenebrous airfield tarmacs of a third-world war zone.

"It's up! We're a go!" our buddy announces, as I finish my second sandwich.

Piling into his SUV, the reality of the situation hits me. *We're doing this. We're about to be homeless. We're about to stow away on an old coal train headed east.* ✸

CHAPTER EIGHT

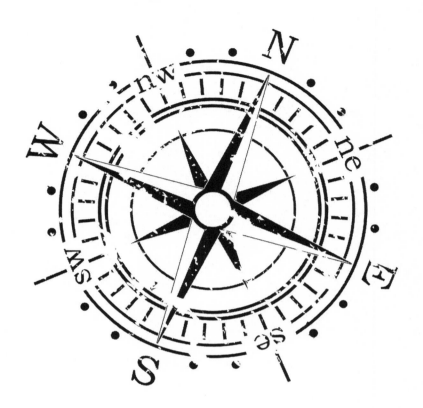

I Still Can't Think
of Anything

"Sometimes, the shit just keeps piling up, while you frantically look for a plunger."—Marty Skovlund

Sitting on the pile of stones, the officer stands over us, still lecturing, and I have to laugh. I'm no longer worried about the consequences. I embrace with delight all of the experiences which brought me here and all the potential for growth stemming from every adventure to come.

We attempt to explain to the officer what we're doing. It seems apparent to him, after less than a minute, that we're not typical train stowaways. The tone of his voice shifts from authoritative to supportive. I can tell he feels bad for pulling us off the train. He can't very well let us back on, but he also doesn't want to put us in jail. In an almost fatherly way, we're directed toward the road and let on our way.

On one hand we failed the initial objective to stow away in the push car of the old coal train, but on the other hand, we won't spend the first twenty-four hours of the mission in a jail cell. Neither of us are very happy, but still excited about every unknown we'll soon encounter. As the sun begins to rise on the first day of the quest, we step off by foot to a gas station from where people frequently hitchhike.

After just three short miles of walking I feel the outside of my right heel and big toe getting hot. It doesn't take being a Ranger to know what's coming next. I know my feet will be hamburger by the end of the day. I made the rookie mistake of buying a brand new pair of boots for the trip, thinking the first five hundred miles will be spent riding the rails, not walking.

At first, hopes are high, but after sitting unassisted for hours with a makeshift cardboard sign asking for a ride east, it's difficult to not feel disappointed. Neither of us look quite clean enough to be trusted, but not yet haggard enough to be in desperate need of help. I suppose there's a sweet spot for receiving charity of this sort, a mark we're both clearly missing.

Staggering numbers of people pass by us, looking away to spare themselves the personal shame of reading our sign and declining their fellow man a helping hand, the way so many people do every day. The way I myself did after a long day at work on any given freeway off-ramp.

Half the morning passes before we finally catch a ride ten miles east to a large truck stop. It isn't the one hop to Kansas City we both envisioned when the trip started, but we're both happy to simply be in motion.

Neither of us are accustomed to asking for help. Our time in the 75th Ranger Regiment ingrained in both of us that asking for help is a sign of weakness. Despite the fact that working as a team is a quintessential part of success in special operations, begging on a street corner is a long stretch from our comfort level.

Nearly an entire day passes, along with hundreds of cars, all ignoring the sign that reads: Two veterans need your help. Going East. Watching people read the sign and pass without pause, makes my blood boil. For years, since leaving the military, I felt as though I was, in certain ways, abandoned by the nation for which I fought. The resume I used with pride proclaiming accomplishments as a medic in Iraq and Afghanistan was passed on by over one-hundred-and-sixty potential employers in the first year after my discharge from the military, a fact that still bothers me. Now here I ask for help and once again I'm passed by.

Enough is enough. It's becoming clear that no random person will help us. The manager of the gas station tells us we're not allowed to fly signs in their parking lot. It's a losing battle. Marty and I decide since no one will pick us up we'll have to get creative. After surveying maps online, Marty notices a railway side-out nearby. A side-out is a section of train track where a train heading west can stop and allow an eastbound train to pass by on a single set of rails, and vice versa. Because of his pre-mission planning, Marty knew that coal trains take the lowest priority and always stop for commuter and cargo trains. If we get lucky a coal train will be headed east while a commuter is going west around that same area.

We leave the truck stop as a few droplets of water land softly on our shoulders. It is a fifteen-minute walk to the side-out. In route we search for hide sights and discuss the best place to mount our attack. A few large pieces of construction equipment are the best we come up with in the otherwise wide-open terrain.

Within moments of dropping our packs behind a rusted out, head high hunk of metal, the wind and rain begin to pick up. An initial search for overhead cover in the area comes up a bust. The rain now pelts down from the north with ferocity. Marty and I tuck ourselves on the southern portion of a massive metal beam which appears to be a part of a future freeway off-ramp.

Marty and I burst into laughter as the wailing tone of a tornado siren alerts everyone within earshot of the imminent approaching danger.

Exposed and surrounded by heavy sharp metal objects, we each bear witness to the altogether terrifying chaotic beauty of our first tornado. A hundred dancers dancing a dozen lifetimes could not hope to mimic nature's graceful pirouetting power unveiling before our eyes. Soaked to the bone, freezing cold, tired and hungry we're still not even eighteen hours into the twenty-one day quest. If this is a sign of things to come, life will be unpleasant for the next three weeks. Yet, through the chaos, we each find our own version of beauty. The now torrential downpour, violent enough to extinguish any fire, ignites the spark of unparalleled adventure in each of us.

The rumbling sound of an incoming train perks our postures. Our lack of experience with such matters makes it tough for us to gauge if we can safely board the moving vessel. Trotting alongside the steel monster on uneven terrain, it quickly becomes apparent that boarding this train safely is impossible.

Two more trains pass while we attempt to seek refuge from the increasingly violent storm. Our barometric ballerina moves like a woman scorned, picking up and fervently propelling cumbersome objects at her whim. The last two trains move far too fast for either of us to grab ahold of, especially under the weight of these cumbersome packs in the slippery wet conditions. We sit in the cold wet rain for hours until both of our cell phone batteries die and my hands and feet are completely numb. I feel an odd sense of familiarity in the situation. Marty suggests heading back toward the truck stop. We can recharge our phones, get warm and see about getting access to a train schedule to improve the chances of catching a ride east.

Drenched, we trudge and slosh our way back to the McDonald's near the gas station where we previously flew our signs. I plug in my phone with frozen fingers and Marty spends the first few dollars of his hundred-dollar budget to purchase two small refillable coffees and a small order of fries. After twenty minutes a traveler stumbles in. His forearms, face and hands are heavily tattooed. The patches on his clothes tell the story of his nomadic lifestyle. Sitting down at the table behind us, he pulls a laptop from his bag. Doing so catches me by surprise. Given his appearance, I'd never guess he owned a computer.

A few minutes after he sits down, the three of us begin conversing.

"Hey, what's up guys? I'm Brian."

Marty and I stand to shake his hand as we introduce ourselves. Brian's body language suggests that most people didn't make the effort to stand up on his account. Marty maintains most of the fifteen-minute conversation with Brian while I continue to search for a way out of town. I check Craigslist rideshare and send messages to people I think could be close.

Brian is exceptionally articulate and kind to both of us. In fact, he's nicer and more helpful than any of the people who passed by us on that street corner today.

A few of Brian's traveling friends enter the fast-food restaurant. They happily invite us into their conversation and provide tips on how to get rides and ask for money.

"You guys gonna finish those fries?" asks one of Brian's friends.

The man asks in such a way that I not only want to give him the fries, but order him a full meal. I don't feel bad for him. It has something to do with the way he asks. It's almost as though he did it in an effort to teach us how to get by.

Since leaving the military I thought I'd asked for help, that I'd screamed for it, for years. It isn't completely clear yet, but what I observe in this moment is: I haven't been going about it the right way. For years, I became increasingly upset because it felt as though my screams for help were ignored, when what I needed to do was stop screaming and start explaining.

The helpful group of misfits departs soon after, leaving Marty and I to continue our effort to find a train headed east. One is set to pass by around 11:00 p.m. and another around 04:00 the next morning.

Around 10:00 p.m. we step off to find a better place to access the trains.

There's nothing at all near the other location except a small ditch. The concern is that the conductor will spot us hiding as the train passes by. It's a risk we have to take. Eleven p.m. comes and goes as we wait. No train.

Shivering and miserable we each refuse to admit to the other how cold we truly are. A pride-filled flashback to the days of our youth. Back to a time when being a man meant being hard, enduring hardship with grit and granite posture. Not the soft version of men who've surrounded us since the start of our assimilation.

The day begins to break and still no train. Completely exposed, we will not be able to stay in this shallow ditch as the sun rises without being spotted. Of course, as soon as we begin to move away from the tracks the train finally comes. Squatting in some tall grass, we wait for our ride to slow down. It doesn't. It passes by at twenty miles an hour.

"We kind of suck at this," Marty says in a half-joking, half-discouraged tone.

"Yeah, that guy with the tattooed face makes it sound so easy," I joke back. Still wet and cold we are now thirty hours into the trip and all of ten miles outside of Denver city limits. The thoughts of failure begin to creep in.

Once again, we try sticking out our thumbs near I-70's eastbound on-ramp. Several more hours go by with no takers. A day closer to the haggard look but still not getting much support from the strangers passing by. There's one group who'd never let us down though. We need reinforcements, we need help from our fellow Rangers.

After a single social media post, multiple men offer to come to our aid. We both place our pride on the back shelf and welcome a ride from an Army recruiter who works for one of our friends. He's only able to get us about thirty miles down the road, but we don't care. We're finally moving and that feels amazing.

Speaking with the young Sergeant feels like not much has changed in the years since I left the military. He isn't sure if he's going to re-enlist or not and isn't sure what he'll do afterward if he decides to get out. It's more common than one might think and can be one of the most detrimental factors to a soldier's return to the civilian world. Marty and I attempt to give him some sage advice. Despite being a good guy, the words seem to fall on deaf ears.

The young Sergeant drops us off at another McDonald's a little further down the road. Marty immediately begins conversing with a few of the patrons sitting in a back corner booth. We share our story with an elderly couple who seems curious about our muddy backpacks. We tell them we're on our second day of an event to benefit people getting out of the military to find jobs and connect with mentors.

"Oh, you two were in the military, huh?"

"Yes, sir."

"Have you seen that one movie, the one with the guys in Afghanistan?"

I know what movie he's talking about. I know the mission he talks about, because I was a part of it. Marty knows what the man is talking about too and takes advantage of the opportunity to apply some of what he learned from the traveling kids in the previous McDonald's.

"You mean *Lone Survivor*? The one about the Navy SEALs?"

"Yeah, yeah, that's the one. We just watched it last night. What did you think about that one?"

Marty knows my feelings about the film. He knows my high degree of disdain for the propaganda machine that takes real world combat situations and bastardizes them to fill seats in theaters. I was outspoken about this fact in an article I wrote which went viral a few months prior, as well as during several radio interviews. I know Marty is about to throw me under the bus, but I also know that my fervent beliefs on the subject have to take a back seat to the mission at hand.

"Well, it's funny that you ask that. Leo here was actually on the recovery mission."

As the elderly couple's eyes widen and shift to me, I'm presented with a choice. I can dive head on into my typical diatribe about the dangers of misleading the public to believe that war is altruistic and a director manipulating history for the sake of profit is an abomination. My other option is to smile and nod, show them pictures that I personally took on that mission which are saved on my iPad and answer whatever questions they may have. I choose the latter.

Without ever having to ask for it, the couple hands Marty a twenty-dollar bill saying, "Breakfast is on us."

I can't be sure if it's because this is our first hot meal in a couple of days or that a couple of people that don't know us, who have no obligation to assist us, so willingly and generously give to our cause, but those hot cakes are so damn good! My overbearing sense of pride slowly fades with each bite.

Marty and I discuss how we're going to get out of the desolate area we now find ourselves in. We know there are Rangers in eastern Colorado who can help us out. We each take to our phones, looking through lists of guys who we know in the area and reach out to them. Within the hour we get lucky and connect with one of the original members of 3rd Ranger Battalion named Hobie, a fixture at all the Ranger events in and around Denver. From some of the stories I've heard him tell, I can tell he's led an adventurous life. He jumps at the opportunity to help us out. ✴

CHAPTER NINE

A Motion Midwest

"No one is useless in this world who lightens the burdens of another."
—Charles Dickens

"You guys need a lift?" Hobie shouts, pulling into the parking lot where Marty and I now lounge, like a couple of professional bums. If Santa Claus packed on a bit more muscle and sported a goatee, instead of a beard, Hobie would be a dead ringer. His laugh is more like a bellow and rings out with consistent frequency. We tell Hobie about another side-out in west Kansas. If he can get us there, we're sure we can make Kansas City. Hobie drives us across the state line, stopping off along the way to buy us a pound of the best fudge in the western United States.

The two-hour car ride ends abruptly with a quick hug and a bid farewell. The cover and concealment in the area is minimal at best. If you've ever travelled in Kansas, you know there's no need to describe different parts of the state. Ninety-nine percent of the place looks exactly the same, flat. We walk down the tracks for a bit, heading away from the small town where the side-out is located. Eventually, we find a few old pallets that we use to fashion a lean-to. The wide-open field in the middle of the country becomes our home for the next fifteen hours as we await a train. We hope and pray for better luck here than our experience during the tornado in Denver. We can only hope that the next train passing by will slow down enough to grab ahold of.

To pass the time, deep philosophical conversations intermix with descriptive tales of past sexual conquests. I've always valued Marty's perspective and admired his concise and intelligent thought process. I'm now beginning to appreciate these qualities further, here, tucked under the gaze of a billion stars. Another frigid night is spent outdoors as we both shiver in discomfort, neither letting the other catch a glimpse of our hardship. We suffer in silence. The porous shelter provides minimal protection from the howling wind, but the fudge and a jar of peanut butter yield a comforting relief for our rumbling stomachs.

One train passes. Too fast. Several hours later, another. As the sun rises over the plains, illuminating the golden fields of anthem-worthy, amber-waving grain, I decide to repack my bag. Two nights ago, in my intoxicated state, I crammed whatever fit, however it would fit.

A single busted flip-flop…my laptop…three pairs of sunglasses…four pairs of boardshorts. *Holy shit, why did I pack half of this crap?*

Each of my earthly possessions lies out in front of me, in several piles. The heat from the early morning sun warms the skin of my back as my shirt hangs draped over my makeshift lean-to in an effort to dry the collected sweat. Just as I pause to observe the perfect tranquility of the moment, the distinctive elongated horn from an inbound coal train shatters the silence of my newfound serenity.

"Are you fucking kidding me?" Marty exclaims as he reaches for his boots and socks drying on a rock. Once again, I shove the random contents back into my over-packed bag in further chaotic fashion.

As the train passes I start to count the time interval between each car using a telephone pole. Four seconds per car, too fast. Now five seconds. Six seconds, "It's slowing down," I call out to Marty. We sit tucked in our hide sight, hearts racing, ready to finally capture the opportunity. We waited for what felt like months for this chance. Seven seconds! "This one is ours." Like the early morning sun, fate too fortuitously shines upon us.

Without the concealment of darkness, or any cover, the two of us dart from our little shanties and sprint for the back of the train. The train slows to a crawl. Grabbing the front rung on the rear car, I pull my eighty-pound bag and myself up to the small runway on the side of the push car. Marty follows shortly after. We both quickly tuck into the engineer compartment and wait.

We wait. We wait some more, and then wait for what feels like a lifetime, for that damn train to take off to the east. All of our chips are on this one hand. Since our drop point is twenty miles south of the middle of nowhere, there's no chance now to hitchhike out of here and walking to the nearest city will take the remainder of our three-week timeline. *We need this, come on we really need this,* echoes through my thoughts.

The cars pull taunt and creep forward. "We're moving!" Marty calls out, exhilarated. The rear car pulls closer to the station where the engineers conduct their shift change. If we pass that point we should be okay. One hundred-and-fifty meters to go. A hundred meters.

"We're close," I tell Marty as I peer through the small grime-covered window. "Less than fifty meters!" Just as the ass end of the train passes by the change point it grinds to a terrifying halt.

"Fuck! Fuck! Fuck! Are you kidding me?"

We have to wait it out. We have no choice. Each of us anticipates the small door opening any second, afraid the engineer may come. Minutes feel like hours. Every heartbeat must be swallowed, the vexatious hollow pump sitting high in my throat drowns out all other sounds. The most important game of hide-and-seek I've been a part of since walking through the mountains of Afghanistan. The feeling of an eminent enemy ambush hangs in the air. A sudden jolt.

The crepitus grinding sound of metal on metal. Then, for whatever reason, the half-mile steel centipede creeps forward once again.

The sense of relief Marty and I both feel is palpable in the stuffy air of the cramped train car. We know that if we make it to Kansas City by nightfall, we'll be okay. I call ahead to a close friend who offers to help us however he can. We've been in contact with the local news channel in Kansas City, hoping to get some much-needed exposure for our cause. Feeling confident in our progress, we set up a tentative live interview for early the next morning. Several times, however, the train creeps to a halt at a side-out or small town, prolonging the journey further.

Nine hours. An agonizing nine hours. Nine hours that feels like sitting in a cramped, grounded airplane motionless on a tarmac without fresh air. At first, the vibrations caused by the ponderous metal wheels is amusing, reminiscent of the buzzing mechanical horse outside of the supermarket we all sat on as children. After nine hours on that horse, however, even the most battle-hardened soldier will beg for a bullet.

Despite the stagnant, stale, stifling air and rigid metallic conditions I can't help but feel remarkably free. A Samuel Clemens moment, if I've ever had one. It's not just the lawlessness that makes the experience exhilarating. The action to me somehow parallels the rebellious, free-spirited nature that the United States of America was born of, that our country was molded by, and that I fear in many ways has lost.

Every agonizing mile we travel means more donations for our fellow veterans. A fact that makes us happy to endure the hardships which accompany the journey. Cell service occurs infrequently at best as the train makes its way through rural Kansas. Marty and I try to keep in contact with our Kansas City contact through text message communication. He's already been driving for an hour and a half to meet us. Neither of us know where the train will stop, so my buddy stages, waiting for instruction.

We know a train yard is coming up and the locomotive will have to slow down as it enters. We discuss the exit strategy and decide the train needs to slow down to at least seven miles per hour before attempting to exit. We also know we don't want to be on that monster when it rolls into the busy train yard. We need to get off before that.

Watching the speedometer drop from 25 to 20, down to 15 then 11 and finally to 7 mph takes about three minutes. The back door seems to be the safest means of egress. Less of a chance to be dragged under and lose a limb. The train chugs and clunks along as Marty and I both try to hide our excitement.

"Keep your feet and knees together, buddy!" Marty jokes, as I prepare to exit first. My mind's eye blinks back to my first exit from a perfectly good aircraft during Army Airborne School. The exhilaration of the moment called martial law over each of my nerves, watching the door to the four-engine turboprop military transport aircraft open, allowing the howling cold swirling wind to smack my face. Now, over a decade later, I find myself knees in the breeze, leaping from another perfectly good means of transportation. Albeit much closer to the stones than the clouds, yet still stimulating an equally exquisite and lasting life experience.

The loose, uneven stones surrounding the rails absorb and separate my feet, forcing me into a running landing. Marty follows close behind with a clamor. Like kids who just threw eggs at a neighbor's house, we dash into the tree line for cover, snickering. Instinctively we each take a knee and immediately begin to scan the surrounding area for any potential threats or anyone who witnessed our exit from our very illegal ride.

"Ohhh fuck!" Marty yells before sprinting toward the train.

What in God's name is he doing?

At a speed I didn't know he's capable of, Marty leaps back at the train. Nearly out of sight, he once again exits the rear door like a paratrooper leaving a C130 Hercules cargo plane.

Running back to the cover position, he informs me through heavy panting breaths, "I forgot my camera, hat and sunglasses on the train."

All I can do is shake my head and think of what Marty was like as a young private in the Army. His six-and-a-half-foot frame, lanky and awkward, before the onset of manhood stuck to his bones.

The sky shifts to myriad vibrant colors, letting us know it will soon be dark. The surrounding crickets drown out our voices with their synchronized chatter, as Marty and I discuss potential rally points to meet with my friend, Matt. Fifty meters behind us is a fence, securing some type of industrial yard. On the other side of the tracks and across the deserted street is a building that looks like a warehouse.

"That may be our only option, Marty."

"Yeah, that looks good. What does that sign say in front?"

"We're going to have to get closer, I can't read it from here."

We emerge from the thick foliage as if we're on a combat patrol. Two teenage boys on bikes coasting down the road slow and stare in disbelief. Marty and I give a casual nod as if to say, "What, you've never seen two Army Rangers appear out of nowhere?"

The smell of the fresh-cut, mid-west grass beneath my feet transports me back to the summers I spent exploring the family farm as a boy. So much has transpired since the carefree days of my youth, yet somehow I feel in this moment, as free and uninhibited as the six-year-old version of myself.

The words on the sign above the building in front of us begin to take shape: The Wild West Gentlemen's Club.

"Well, if that isn't a sign, I don't know what is, Martin! That looks like a perfect place for Matt to meet us. Plus, I'm thirsty after that long ride."

Within minutes of notifying Matt of our location, an old green Ford pickup truck pulls up to where we sit on the roadside. I haven't seen Matt in close to ten years. As he hops out of the truck, his smile beams through the years added to his face. A long hug is the only way to greet a brother with whom you fought in two wars. I was Matt's medic in both Iraq and Afghanistan. We made the rank of Sergeant together. We walked side by side in the mountains of the Kunar Province as well as the dark streets of Tikrit. How many times did we narrowly evade death by each other's side?

Matt isn't what most people think of when they envision a special operations soldier. Most people have some false concept of a muscle-bound, meathead model type. Perhaps we can thank the movies for that false representation, or maybe blame our childhood action figures. Regardless, most of the men I worked with were built for mission success, not for winning figure contests. Trim and wiry. Confident. Stepping softly with an unparalleled capacity for violence subdued beneath a glass surface. Matt epitomizes such demeanor. His sunken, steely eyes set to a distant, almost removed stare. Tattoos cover most of his exposed skin and while his lean figure may not appear imposing to the unaware, I know firsthand what he's capable of under attack.

"Doc! How the fuck are you?"

"Well, I smell like a dead hooker and just spent nine of the most mind-numbing hours of my life staring at wheat from the back of a coal train we just jumped off of.... How the fuck are you?"

Matt responds with a laugh and asks, "Are you guys thirsty?" As though we share one mind, we all have the same idea. Simultaneously, we look at the only establishment in eyesight, then back to each other.

"I'm buying," is all Matt says, as we place our packs into the cab of his truck. To call the place a seedy establishment is generous. It's late in the afternoon on a Tuesday, not a time when most strip clubs have their "A" players on the floor. A fact that does nothing to dissuade us from entering the dank, windowless building.

A three-dollar cover charge is a sign of terrible things to come. Matt doesn't have any cash on hand, so I pay the nine-dollar entrance fee for the three of us. It's the first time I dip into my hundred-dollar budget since our departure. A fitting use of funds, if you ask me.

"Look man, I'll buy the beer," Matt says in a way suggesting nothing at all had changed since our time together in the military. I just shake my head in response to the crooked grin plastered on his face. I know he's more than good for it, but making fun of each other without saying a word is a long tradition between guys like us. Matt buys a round of light domestic bottled beer. Marty and I omit such a foul stench even I'm offended to be in our presence.

The soggy pungent odor of cheap perfume and shame lays languid in the air like fog on a London street. The large round wooden table beside the stage is as good a place as any to commence our overdue reunion. Two guys in their early twenties sit quietly a few tables away. The five of us comprise the entire audience for the limber, late-thirty-something who clearly benefits heavily from the poor lighting in this place.

The hardships Marty and I endured to arrive here all seem worth it, as I begin to reconnect with an old friend. Following the dismal performance, the aged dancer makes her way off stage and intrusively interrupts Matt mid-sentence, "You guys want to tip me for my dance or what?"

That's a bold approach, I think to myself as she obnoxiously leans into our conversation.

"Well, we'd love to, but you see we're on a bit of a fixed budget," Marty explains with the delivery and tact of a veteran politician.

"What the fuck are you doing in a strip club then asshole?" she mutters as she walks away.

"Gentlemen's club!" I shout as she waddles into the darkness. The next solicitor is not so easily dissuaded. When she refuses to leave, Matt pulls out the four crumpled dollars he received back from the bartender for the beers he bought.

"If I give you this, will you go away?"

As soon as the money shifts from his hand to hers, then her hand to her G-string she looks to Marty for an equal payout. Once again he explains, "We're not in a position financially to tip you." When she refuses to leave, Marty takes the opportunity to tell her about the mission we're on.

"Oh, my God! I feel so bad for being shitty to you guys! My son is in the military and I totally respect what you are doing."

"Your son? You have a son in the military?" Matt asks in shock. "How fucking old are you?"

"I'm in my forties."

"Damn, you're doing alright for forty."

"It's the fake tits."

"Okay, I see that."

Like some kind of a hidden camera joke, she asks us collectively, "Have you seen the movie *Lone Survivor?*" A grin consumes Marty's face. I know he's going to throw me under the bus again. This time, however, I can defer to my amigo Matt since he was there, too.

As quickly as "Well, Leo was a medic on that mission," slips out of Marty's mouth, I deflect, "Well, Sanders was a team leader on that mission."

She looks at us in a combination of disbelief and bewilderment.

"Now I really feel bad! I can't take this money from you guys. Here take it back." When Matt refuses to take the four dollars from the woman's frayed undergarment she turns to Marty, placing the ball of filthy paper in his hand.

"Use this on your trip. I've got to get backstage, but thank you guys for what you're doing. I think it's great."

"Marty, do you realize what just happened."

"What? No, what's up?"

"Marty, you just defied physics and all rules of the natural order of the world!"

"Come again?"

"Marty, a stripper just tipped YOU...in a strip club. That. Just. Happened!"

The rest of the evening unravels in the typical fashion of a couple of old Army buddies reuniting after years apart. In a dark basement bar in Kansas City we swap old stories and new. I take advantage of the opportunity to plug my phone into the single, free outlet behind the bar. The way it does, one beer evolves into those two fateful words, "Last call!"

Stumbling up the cobblestone stairs and onto the sidewalk, we observe the collective mass exodus of the other bars onto the popular Kansas City street.

"Son of a bitch!"

"What?"

"My phone. I forgot my damn phone!"

The door had already shut and locked behind us. Any other day I'd say forget it and come back in the morning. We don't have that option this time. We have a live television interview in a couple of hours, then have to be on our way east shortly afterward. Pounding on the front door like a sheriff serving a warrant does nothing but make my hand sore. The two people closing the place down are downstairs in that dungeon of a pub.

"I think there may be a backdoor," Matt chimes in.

He's right; a narrow corridor leads down toward a door behind the building. It looks as though this entrance will be right about where the actual bar is. I try knocking, which escalates to frantic pounding on the flimsy door. Nothing.

A few minutes of thumping pass before I actually reach for the handle. Nope. Wait, yep, a quick kick and...that does it. The door flings open and without hesitation, I lunge through. And this is how felonies happen. Three steps in, grab the phone, three steps out. A quick sprint up the alleyway and, "Let's get out of here!"

"What? Did you get it?"

"Yeah, but we should go."

"Do I want to know?"

"You sure don't, Marty!"

It's a short ride to a late night diner. We all agree that black coffee and pancakes will help counter the effects of the IPAs we rehydrated with, before making the live television appearance.

Even at three in the morning, the rundown Kansas City diner bustles with activity. The three of us choose a booth seat. We quickly notice the loud group telling stories in the corner behind us. Before I can even order a coffee, Matt interjects himself into the group's conversation. They're all a few years younger than us. I instantly observe Matt's interest in the brunette girl seated in the middle seat. By the time our coffee arrives we somehow manage to slide into their booth and join their party. Less than amused, the two guys accompanying the girl seem to be unfamiliar on how to handle an alpha male like Matt. They have no recourse. In as blatant of a way as I've ever seen, Matt continues to make advances at who I can only assume is one of their girlfriends. The swoop occurs right in front of them, and with exception to the dejected look plastered on each of their faces, no one objects.

Just before our soggy, late-night meal arrives, the power goes out. "Looks like someone didn't pay their electric bill," Matt announces, in a surly tone. Despite my happy buzz from the beer Matt bought, I'm becoming a little concerned about the time. I'm not sure how far away we are from the television station where we're supposed to give our interview.

I have to admire how persistent Matt is with this girl. When one advance doesn't work, he tries another, and another until it's time to leave. A war of attrition I'm sure he'd win if we didn't have to leave.

Graciously, he pays for our meal and we head out into the brisk early summer morning to the sounds of a homeless man screaming to himself, stumbling down the sidewalk across from the diner.

We have an hour before our appearance and Matt assures me that we're only twenty minutes away. As we stagger back to his old pickup truck I see the muscles of his face drop in the dim light of the flickering street lamp.

"What? What's wrong?"

"The keys. They're. I. I locked them in the truck."

Without hesitation, the three of us revert back to our previous selves. As though a tire on one of our Humvees blew out on a mission, we have to get the vehicle back in play as quickly as possible. No worry or complaint, just action. We have a limited amount of time to gain access to the truck. Calling a locksmith will take too long. Aside from the loud homeless man across the street, the area is deserted. I pull out my pocketknife and attempt to pry the sliding rear window open. The blade I carried for years snaps under the returning force. Marty and Matt scour the surrounding area for something to use to pick the lock.

Forty-five minutes until our interview.

Matt emerges from behind the diner with his trademark-crooked smile, and an old hanger.

"Do you know how to break into a truck with one of those?" I ask.

"What's that supposed to mean, Doc? Like I'm a criminal or something?"

"Well…do you?"

"Yeah, but I don't like your insinuation."

"You've broken into cars before haven't you?" Marty chimes in.

"Look guys, you're missing the point here," Matt responds, as he forms a perfect hook out of the wire hanger and inserts it beneath the driver's side window.

Thirty-five minutes until our interview.

A fidget, a twist, a slight grunt and then, POP. The sound of the lock clicking open is beautiful. Anticipating the comments from Marty and I, Matt just tosses the hanger in the back of the truck, not looking at either of us, mumbling, "Shut up, both of you."

Even though we're only twenty minutes away and have a half an hour to get there, Matt drives like a man possessed. He isn't going to be the reason we miss this interview. We arrive at the station with enough time to enjoy another cup of coffee in the lobby before going on air. I hadn't noticed the height difference between Marty and I until someone at the station suggests I stand on a box for the segment. During the interview, Marty takes over and answers the questions with the grace and composure of a veteran PR guy. I, on the other hand, am not as fluid, concentrating the majority of my effort on not accidentally saying the F-word on live television.

Following the interview, Matt brings us back to his house where, for the first time in days, we're able to sleep under the cover of a roof. Two hours. That's how much time we have before we have to move on. It's just enough sleep to remind each of us how tired we are. While we sleep, Matt's father takes it upon himself to buy a ticket for Marty and I on an eastbound Amtrak train. The train tickets are to Saint Louis and departing soon. We have just enough time to stop off for a plate of world famous Bar-B-Que at Arthur Bryant's before being dropped off at the train station. ✸

CHAPTER TEN

Tired Eyes and Heavy Hearts

"There are many truths of which the full meaning cannot be realized until personal experience has brought it home."—John Stuart Mill

Marty and I agree this train is a vast improvement from the last one we traveled on. Marty and I are both exhausted and look forward to getting a couple more hours of sleep. That, however, is not possible. There's a significant increase in traffic on the site we set up for donations. Messages offering assistances and places to stay along our trip fill our inboxes. We have messages from other news stations requesting interviews. As we squeak and rock down the tracks headed for Missouri, Marty and I take the opportunity to answer as many messages as we can.

By the time we arrive at the next station, I can barely keep my head up. We make arrangements to stay with another friend who I served with in the Army. The excitement of seeing another old friend is like a shot of espresso to my otherwise drained body. I can't help but smile seeing Justin. His face now covered with a scruffy beard, yet otherwise unchanged from the days of his military service.

I want desperately to stay up all night catching up with him in his kitchen, drinking the beers waiting for us. I want to know how life has treated him since he left the military. My body is drained, though. Shortly after inhaling the giant hamburgers he prepares for us, Marty and I both succumb to our exhaustion.

Every muscle seems locked in place as I force my heavy eyelids open the next morning. Six hours of sleep on an old couch is the most rest we've had in five days. Justin drives us out of town to a gas station where we arranged a ride with a guy who's followed our journey online. Justin buys us each a bagel, gives a quick hug and hands us off to a gentleman who neither of us has met before.

The stranger agrees to take us toward Indianapolis where another former Ranger said he'd meet us. A couple more hours passing through the cornfields of the Midwest, another quick gas station hand off and the backseat of another pickup truck. Marty and I finally feel like we're making up for the time we lost sitting out the tornado waiting for a train.

Our movement begins receiving more and more attention through the media. We receive a message stating that if we make it to New York City by the 20th there will be two one-way tickets to Bergen, Norway, waiting for us. At the pace we're now moving, this actually seems like a possibility. Marty and I begin mapping out how many miles we have to travel each day in order to make it in time. Simultaneously, we receive more requests to make television and radio appearances. The next one will happen in downtown Indianapolis the following morning. Jeff, the former Ranger who picks us up somewhere in western Indiana, offers us a place to stay for the night and a hot meal. Jeff is already helping us so much more than he has to. I feel like I'm imposing terribly when I ask, "Can you take us downtown at four thirty tomorrow morning for another interview?"

Without hesitation he says, "No problem. Looks like I better stop drinking now, though."

By the time we confirm the interview, it's midnight. I spend the last two hours debating the feminist hypocrisy of requiring a man to put the toilet seat down with Jeff's amazing wife. Ranger's wives are a special breed.

Most wives wouldn't even entertain the idea of, "Hey honey, two guys whom you've never met are going to be staying at our place tonight. We're going to feed them, let them drink our beer, and the loquacious one is going to want to have a drunken debate until the sun comes up."

Our second live interview goes better than the first. It's still dark outside when we finish. Jeff agrees to take us all the way to Columbus, Ohio. In exchange for his hospitality, I give him a short private coaching session in his garage on the fundamentals of Olympic weightlifting. As small of a thing as it is, it makes me feel a lot better about the situation. I feel like I am, in a very small way, giving something in return.

It's still very difficult for Marty and I to ask for help. We're being forced out of our comfort zone on this trip in more ways than one. The nearly insurmountable amount of pride we both carry has to dissolve if we're going to be successful on this quest. Our fellow veterans depend on us to get as far as possible. The only way that will happen is if we humble ourselves and ask for help.

I arrange a place to stay in Columbus from an unlikely host. A few months back when Adam produced a copy of my first book in Santiago, Chile, for me to sign he said, "Keep in touch."

I politely responded, "Absolutely," knowing that the chances I'd ever see him again after that weekend were pretty slim.

When Adam sees we're heading toward Ohio, he insists upon helping us. Life is strange like that. Adam arranges a hotel room for

Marty and I, which is way above and beyond what we expect. Jeff drops us off at the front door of the hotel, wishes us luck and makes the long drive back to Indianapolis alone.

To say we're out of place under the chandelier, leaning against the mahogany desk to sign in, is an understatement. We haven't showered or slept in a real bed since our trek began. The odor cloud following us into the lobby is close to visible.

Marty and I wait in the lobby for nearly a half hour for our room to be cleaned. The chairs we sit in could be made of stone, we don't notice, we sink into them making every effort to prevent our eyes from closing. Fighting the sleep monster, I feel as though I've somehow returned to Miss Cherney's eighth-grade math class. Why they even bother trying to teach algebra after lunch is beyond me.

Our room feels like a regal palace. It takes ten minutes standing under the high-powered hot stream of water in the shower to remove the week's worth of grime accumulated on my tired body. The next order of business is to slip on a pair of shorts and slide between the cool fresh-pressed sheets for a long overdue rest. Before the four-inch thick comforter settles, I fall into a deep REM3 sleep state.

"Hey…Leo…. Wake up!"

"Huh, what? Is it seven?"

"No man, you've only been asleep for about twenty minutes."

"Why the fuck are you? What? Dude…piss off!"

"The local news station called. They want to interview us for the evening news."

"When? What? I don't care."

"Come on man, we've got work to do."

He's right. This is about getting as much exposure as possible for the cause and we can't refuse a primetime interview just because we're tired. Begrudgingly, I peel myself from the king-sized utopia, slip into the same pair of green cargo pants I travelled in, and grab my backpack. Those pants, so sweat-saturated filthy, could stand up by themselves at this point, and crunch as I press my legs through.

Right as we finish the interview, Adam pulls into the hotel parking lot. Adam still works for Rogue Fitness as a project manager. His entire team pulled together resources to chip in for our hotel room and offers to take us out to an absolutely amazing dinner. A little calorically depleted, we take advantage of the opportunity.

Marty and I are taken aback by the generosity they show us. Adam is also a military veteran and believes strongly in the mission we're on. After dinner we watch the broadcast of the interview Marty and I did earlier in the day with the entire crew.

A couple of Adam's coworkers invite us to an all-you-can-eat pancake breakfast at the local American Legion the next morning. Adam graciously offers to come to the hotel, pick us up and take us to the event. Part of me wants to decline and spend a few extra hours in that bed, but the other part of me, the stronger part, doesn't turn down all-you-can-eat pancakes.

The next morning arrives like a sixteen year old having his first sexual experience, too soon. *Pancakes. Think about the pancakes, Leo. Think about that tall stack of hotcakes. Keep moving forward. I am so tired. What a perfect night sleep I just had,* the kind you don't want to leave behind. The kind you continue to think about well into the following afternoon.

Snapping and waving in the Ohio breeze, hundreds of tiny American flags line the mile of suburban road leading to the American Legion. A perfect painting of the American dream, no longer the focus of most media outlets, sprawls before my eyes. I gaze upon children playing in freshly cut lawns as their parents look on from their front porches. Encapsulated and frozen in time, on this street I see with my own heavy eyes what the U.S. must have looked like in the 1950's.

The time warp doesn't end when we arrive. As Marty and I step from Adam's car we both notice an extravagant display on the front lawn of the Legion building; a restored Army green jeep from World War II, a series of uniforms displayed in chronological order and several people dressed as soldiers from past wars. The event is much more than either of us expected. At the front door stand a half-dozen women in their early to mid-twenties dressed like pinups from the 40's and 50's. For the first time in my life, I'm fully distracted from all-you-can-eat pancakes.

In awe, Marty and I revel in the history laid out before us. Uniforms worn by Rangers who stormed the beach on D-day are presented in pristine condition. We have the fortune to speak with several veterans.

Marty and I are introduced to a man who served as a UDT diver in the Korean War. Some kyphotic shell encapsulates the old warrior. A grey blemished tint of seasoned armor. One of the forefathers to the modern-day Navy SEALs, he shows an initial hesitation toward speaking to us. As the sun breaks through the clouds, chasing the morning chill from my exposed arms, the distance in years dissolves between us. Unbeknown to all others in attendance, a simple introduction twists a rusted lever on the fountain of youth. He's taller now than just moments ago, transported to his prime. No longer an old lone warrior amidst the flock of sheep.

The decades between his time in combat and ours disappear and suddenly we're just three veterans sharing our experiences. A chronicle of novels in love and war could be constructed from the narrative of our twenty-minute conversation. A bridge built across generations and secured by common experience. Not just war, but all the sleepless nights since when we laid awake, pretending to be like everyone else, those blessed and unafflicted souls.

When people at the function overhear what Marty and I are doing, we're greeted with wave upon wave of enthusiastic handshakes and thank you's. A ten-year-old boy hands me a crumpled up five-dollar bill, which he saved, stating simply, "I hope this helps your trip."

His eyes, so pure, unstained by the barrage of political opinion, fear mongering, and antipathy-laden diatribes of this side versus the other. They just look up at me with candid appreciation. And I look down through salt-blurred vision, yet impeccable lucidity. Now I see so clearly what I could not see before.

For years, I maintained a misguided feeling of abandonment from the country that asked me to go to war. I felt no one cared, that my struggles were just that, mine. In a single morning, a fault line fractures under my long-held opinion, sending them falling to fissure. ❀

CHAPTER ELEVEN

Brothers Beyond Birth

"The greatest minds are capable of the greatest vices as well as the greatest virtues."—Rene Descartes

I'm sure I am not the only one to have observed how, in life, we gravitate toward certain individuals. No matter how far removed we become geographically, we're drawn back to them, those interesting and intersecting pieces of our own persona. It's no surprise to me when Marty and my journey bring us to the front porch of a longtime friend named Matt Voll. We served as Army medics together a decade earlier. Following our time in the military we became college roommates. We always made it a point to stay in touch. He'd always been a kind of older brother to me.

Even among Rangers, Matt's antics are legendary. Tales of him kidnapping a midget at a bar and getting drunk and running with the bulls in Spain or ensuring I'd never be allowed back into the University of Notre Dame are blurbs on a long list of Matt's debauchery accomplishments. I had the privilege of standing as a groomsmen at his wedding a few years earlier, but had yet to meet his new daughter.

Matt graduated from medical school and owns a house outside of Cleveland, Ohio.

The familiar devious beaming grin plastered on his face as I enter his new home, without knocking, is a long overdue sight. Set like land mines across the floor, toddler-friendly toys replace the randomly strewn, empty beer cans of the homes Matt and I shared. The aroma of stale pizza and musty gym shirts give way to potpourri and baby formula. *Still the same Matt Voll,* I think, *just in a different environment.* Then I see it. I see my battle-hardened, best friend scoop up the fuzzy-pink creature swaying at his feet and commence to speak to it in a foreign language comprised of goo-goo's and ga-ga's.

This can't be the same guy. This can't be the same man who drank three bottles of red wine at that Italian restaurant and demanded a fourth bottle from a hesitant manager. This can't be the same guy who willingly volunteered for me to sew the back of his split head with fishing line and a hook in Panama City, Florida. As I begin to wonder if I'm in the right house, he sets the little rosy-cheeked crea-ture on the center island of the kitchen next to all the knives, walks over to me with open arms and says, "Let's get fucked up!" *That's the Matt Voll I know!*

Marty and I embrace the much-needed tactical pause in the com-pany of old friends, Irish whiskey and more grilled meat than a pla-toon of soldiers can eat. One old story flows to the next as the late night evolves into the early morning. Anchors for eyelids, the gru-eling pace of the trip thus far creates a new reality. My exhaustion surpasses my desire to catch up with an old friend. I pardon myself from the conversation and slip quietly into the fresh cold sheets of one of Matt's guest rooms. The anchors hold tight until well past morning light.

News media engagements fill the next day. A gallon of coffee and a pound of bacon provided by our hosts acts as fuel for the myri-ad of questions Marty and I answer from local news personalities regarding our mission. By this point, the nation is interested in two former Army Rangers going nomad for a noble cause. The objective is to get as far as possible, but really we're really raising awareness for our fellow veterans struggling with their own assimilations back into civiliandom. Marty and I happily embrace the opportunity to be a voice for our brothers.

We return to Matt's home and accept his offer to wash our filthy clothes. His duties as an emergency room doctor pull him away from our impromptu reunion, leaving us to progress onward. Parting ways, I gain a new respect for a man whom I didn't believe my respect could be any greater. The greatest juggling act that I've yet to attempt; a wife, a child, a career, a home, and a storied past of victory and folly alike. Like Kyle, he had it all. Perhaps he didn't know it, but he had it all.

And like an arrow drawn from the quiver of familiarity and fired wildly to the winds, we push east, unsure of the location of our next impact.

Within a few hours we arrive at the home of another former Ranger. Social media is becoming one of our strongest allies on this journey and we milk it for all it's worth. Despite never having met our new host before, Peter welcomes Marty and I into his home with open arms. What I find in our gracious host's home fuels a fear in me, one which burned for years before Marty and my departure.

The American dream. The coveted endgame of every nine-to-fiver. White picket fence, two point three kids, steady job, retirement plan, spouse, mortgage, and a general malaise for your own disposition. As a culture we chase it. Security. Possessions. Status. By modern American standards, Peter is winning. In fact, if you look at the living conditions of most middle-class families the world over, he sits firmly in the top one percent. Despite that, over beers and another massive plate of grilled meat, sitting on his back porch his tone gives tell to a different reality. A longing for days past, nostalgia for the long since buried version of himself when he was among the world's elite. The life he lived in the mid 80's is a page out of my own book, circa 2005.

Decades later his perspective is a potential crow's nest, so I sit and intently listen. There's no regret in his mildly slurred speech, just a longing for days past and an intense memory of the person he thought he'd be at this time. And with that unfulfilled memory, a unique sadness creeps in.

By my father and his father's standard, Pete has won. He owns a nice two-story home in the suburbs, has beautiful healthy children, a marriage and maintains a steady income. However, Marty and my presence shakes something loose in this old warrior. Perhaps he sees the fire in our eyes burning for a cause larger than us. Perhaps he envies our adventure or perhaps he's slipped into one of the toughest places to get out of, the mind. "The mind is it's own place, it can make a heaven out of hell or hell out of heaven." A simple, yet poignant, quote etched on the inside of a bathroom wall at a specific Special Operations selection site, no doubt borrowed from Mr. John Milton. Somehow, living a seemingly parallel existence to Kyle and Matt has yielded a completely different disposition in Pete. As if some sort of universal happiness algorithm exists.

It isn't the institution of marriage or commitment to another life that frightens me. I'm simply not interested in building a suburban utopia, I know that about myself. My personal terror has long been comfort. In comfort we seem to forget the frostbite sting of our previous struggles and all the hell we walked through to find warmth. If you're going to spend a lifetime building a heaven, first make sure it isn't hell, then look back frequently and remember why you grabbed the first brick.

In a now-familiar fashion, our time with Peter is both informative and short-lived. He drives us a staggering five hours across the state of Pennsylvania to link up with an Air Force veteran by the name of Kerry Patton.

Kerry, like Marty and myself, has a decent following as a writer. His pragmatic and logical approach to prose makes him an author I admire. I'm excited to meet him. The appropriate exchange location of a bar is set. In an almost fatherly way, Peter hands us over to Kerry. We all share a beer together and we push east as Pete returns west.

Within forty-five minutes the three of us pull up to Kerry's farmhouse. The crunch of stone under his truck tires on the gravel driveway creates a *déjà vu*-like memory of arriving to my grandparent's farm in upstate New York as a child.

The smell of damp grass and freshly-split wood permeates the air. The cluck of chickens and honk of geese is a welcome reprise from the obtrusive bellow of car horns and pungent nasal attack of recent cities visited.

Despite all the comfort in this serene environment, a familiar thirst arrives with new intensity. For over a week, every drink I consumed someone else provided. The stipulations of this game I'm playing confines me to a more stringent budget than I'm used to. Furthermore, to tap into the hundred-dollar allowance would take resources from my brethren.

For the first time in my life, a general desire gives way to a legitimate craving. A man I look up to shows me around his home, his personal castle, and the only thought racing through my simple mind is, *Please, God, tell me this man has alcohol at his house.*

I hadn't recognized it before because, flawlessly, we were handed a libation by each of our previous hosts. The beer drunk an hour ago turns something on in me. The intense craving dulls my senses. All of a sudden and seemingly out of nowhere, my need for a drink supersedes every other priority.

I don't have to wait long. One of Kerry's hobbies is brewing beer. One after another I consume his various concoctions. Each one more satisfying than the last. I hear the voice of reason screaming after me, "You've flown far too high, now you're too close to the sun." I flap harder and higher with every indulgent taste. I do not fear the addiction, I embrace it. Let the fire of my madness swell and it will warm the world. Knowing, as Jagger said, "Anything worth doing is worth overdoing."

Great men are not made by way of moderation. Those poets, musicians, athletes, entertainers, and all who we've come to admire never capitulated to temperance. Their iron forged in the fire of excess. To be weak is to give in. To be strong is to abstain completely, but to be great is to indulge in all the pleasures and pains of life, to swim through the drowning tumult and turbulence and fear. Those poor and timid souls who cower in the face of their own temptations will never experience the exaltation of plummeting to the sea, swimming hard against the current and making their way to shore, exhausted, exuberant, alive.

The next morning I awake, and am given ten minutes to be ready to leave. The night before we set up a radio interview and will stop at the studio on our way out of town. Additionally, Kerry uses his contacts to establish two other high-profile interviews in New York City the day after tomorrow. All we have to do is get to the city, which like us, never seems to sleep.

The interview and proceeding trip to New York is uneventful. Marty and I have our dialogue dialed in at this point. We indulge in coffee and donuts courtesy of our new good friend Mr. Patton. The XM radio in his truck provides a dance-worthy soundtrack for the next few hours of smooth highway travel. Moving by way of our veteran network has become almost routine. Kerry personally drives us to West Point Military Academy in upstate New York. At a McDonald's just off post we meet up with a George Clooney-esk, Lieutenant Colonel named Charles Faint who insists we call him Charlie.

Handshakes and soft-serve ice cream seals the hand off. Marty and I hop into Charlie's lifted red jeep and roll into one of the most prestigious campuses in the United States. The historical significance of this place is not lost on either of us. The towering stone buildings silently tell the story of housing and educating generations of some of the greatest leaders in the nation's history.

Our vibrant enthusiasm quickly morphs into somber respect as we approach the West Point Cemetery. Row upon row of granite waves echo a commitment to something greater and a willingness to sacrifice every tomorrow. There's no way to slouch in a moment like this. The pride, the stoic gratitude won't allow it. Walking through the rows and reading the names gives lift to each of our brows and an openness to our chests. There's no pity here, just honor.

Charlie's home is located on the military base. As Marty and I enter, I notice that the theme is consistent. Charlie's home is well kept, yet subtle traces of children linger about. The drawings on the refrigerator, the basket of tiny pink shirts outside of the laundry room, and the toys out back all tell the story of another happy suburban family.

Early the next morning we receive a ride to the train station and enough cash to pay the fare. The southbound train rumbles toward New York City where we're set to give a few radio interviews. ✤

CHAPTER TWELVE

Bergens Beyond

"Do you want to know who you are? Don't ask. Act!
Action will delineate and define you."—Thomas Jefferson

Arriving at Grand Central Station is as grand an experience as the name suggests. My mind flips through the catalog of movies that used this location as a backdrop. Despite having never been here, there's a comforting familiarity. We momentarily become actors in the midst of a great role. That comfort vanishes quickly as Marty and I step into the chaos of the Manhattan street.

We swim through an endless school of frantic fish, attempting to make our way a dozen blocks to the XM radio headquarters. Arguably, the greatest city ever erected omits its own unique buzz of clamor and hustle. The stench of day-old trash permeates and lingers in the air. My neck quickly grows tired from snapping left and right, attempting to keep up with the overwhelming flood of stimulation. Men in suits all but step on the lower class, in rapid route to another merger, another acquisition of perceived power, and the snatching of arbitrary stacks of paper. A modern-day Tikal, pulsating in its prime.

Blissfully unaware of the necessity of its eventual collapse and dissolution into a fine black ink on the pages of history.

We enter the lobby and proceed up to the twenty-somethingth floor where we're met by the show's producer and mutual friend, Ian. Jokingly, Ian remarks how we both look homeless, chuckling to himself and guiding us through a maze of chest-high cubicles. He shows us to the much-needed free coffee and gives us the rundown of the show. We have nearly an entire hour to speak about what we're doing, a fact that elates both Marty and myself.

Ian introduces us to the host of the show, Andrew, and we get comfortable. As Andrew introduces us on the air, there's a distinct tone to his voice. Unlike some of the other people who interviewed us in the past week, he truly seems to care about our cause. During the interview, Andrew takes out his wallet and proceeds to remove every last dollar and hands it to us, apologizing it's not more. The gesture fills me with gratitude and humility, following the years believing veterans were underappreciated. After the show Andrew calls his friend, Emmet, who owns an Irish pub a few blocks away and tells him about what we're doing. We have several hours to kill between the end of Andrew's show and the beginning of the next one with no place to go. Without having met us, Emmet happily agrees to host us at his restaurant.

Not once do our pint glasses reach the three-finger mark before a new one is delivered. The hospitality of Emmet and his staff makes us feel like A-list celebrities. A simple phone call from Andrew explaining we're veterans in need of a little help is all that's required to send the staff of the already busy Irish pub into overdrive.

The world blurs by the time Marty and I excuse ourselves for our second radio interview. The compounding effects of a plethora of adult libations served in alternating sequence; beer, whiskey, beer, whiskey, and so on, sets spin to the world external. The brilliant burning bright lights of Manhattan at night swirl and melt together in a Technicolor kaleidoscope of inebriated bliss and childlike amusement. The blocks move faster this time.

"The bar tab in that place would've been more than our entire budget for this trip, Marty."

"I know. We're gonna have to remember to send them something. What an...hiccup...awesome guy!"

We arrive back at the same building, take the elevator to the same floor and end up in the same studio where we were a few hours earlier. This time, however, our inhibitions are squelched. Liquid courage flows through each of our veins. Firmly and assertively we greet our host and pull up our seats. Despite knowing less about David Webb's show, Marty and I both exude a confidence gained from having delivered so many interviews.

By the first intermission, it's clear we have our host's attention. We're concise with our now-well-practiced message. We educate David's audience on the importance of maintaining purpose and connection post-military. We inform them about the mission of the GallantFew, providing mentorship to recently discharged veterans, pairing them with individuals of a similar caliber who've been out of the military for a few years and are now established. We implore anyone who may be apprehensive, yet in a position to hire a veteran, to give their application a second look, pointing out a long list of general qualities learned in the military, which are highly beneficial in the workplace.

Pushing the mic away from his face during commercial break, David asks, "Do you enjoy bourbon?" It's difficult for me to hide my excitement in moments like this. I don't even have to respond verbally. David signals his assistant in the sound booth and has him go get an unopened bottle of bourbon. He pours Marty and I each a healthy glass as we answer a question from a caller.

By the end of the hour, David invites us to dinner. We meet him at a steakhouse that neither Marty nor myself is appropriately dressed for. In all honesty, by this point in our trip, we aren't dressed for Burger King. Under the weight of our tattered backpacks and stench cloud, we enter Del Frisco's. The welcome we receive from the modelesque hostess suggests that David called ahead and told them we were coming. He finishes up with the show and will meet us shortly. The gorgeous blonde motions to take our bags to check in the coat room, a notion I can't help but laugh at. Not because of the irony of having my old Kelty sitting next to a bunch of thousand-dollar coats in a swanky New York City steakhouse, more the suspicion turned truth when she attempts to shoulder the overstuffed pack.

"How much does this…did you carry…what is in this thing?"

"Please, you don't have to…"

She interrupts me in that way a prideful woman will, "No, I've got it," as she drags, rather than carries, the cumbersome object into the closet. Guided to our seats, Marty and I devour the free bread, while we wait for David to arrive.

In a most gracious way, David indulges his two homeless combat veteran companions with the finest steak dinner that either of us ever experienced. In as low flash a way as possible, he spares no expense. When it's time to leave he asks his personal driver to take us to our next destination, the home of a friend living in New York City named Jack Murphy. Jack's course of action after his time in the military made him a role model of mine. We served in 3rd Ranger Battalion around the same time.

When I left the military, Jack went on to earn his green beret and serve in Special Forces. More impressively, he later went on to become a renowned author and editor of the website where I got my start as a writer.

Jack is another guy who doesn't quite fit the description of what most people think of when you mention Army Ranger and Green Beret. The common stereotype of a muscle-bound caveman willing and able to crush rocks with their hands is really more exception than rule. Jack, like many men in Special Operations is well spoken, intelligent and highly analytical.

Jack has always been a stand up guy, a fact further proven by his willingness to open his home to two vagrants. A beer or two later and Marty and my ability to provide engaging company comes to an anticlimactic halt. Exhaustion bites hard leaving us both drooling on Jack's couch cushions.

We step off before Jack wakes up the next morning, a movement that really digs at me. Despite crashing in his living room, I don't get to ask him all the questions I want to. Questions like how he made the transition from warrior to writer, how his experience in graduate school is treating him, and his future writing projects. Mission first, though.

We have one more television engagement before heading further east, further from our point of origin and closer to raising money and awareness for veteran assimilation issues.

Airport atmospheres are cyclones of anxiety, joy, hustle, and sorrow. A tempest of emotion all swirl together in recycled air. All, but the latter, fills Marty and I as we stand in line at the Norwegian Airlines counter. Due to a generous donor, we shift our plans. We receive an email confirmation of the tickets bought by someone sympathetic to our cause but neither of us, standing in that serpentine line, have any certainty we'll actually be able to board the plane. Our initial plan was to try to find a boat captain willing to take us on board. In return for day labor we'd receive a ride as far into the Atlantic Ocean as time permitted. Now we inch closer to the ticket counter of a previously unknown airline in hopes we'll soon board a plane.

The three beautiful twenty-something women behind us grab my attention. Approaching the counter, passport in hand, Marty and I present a screenshot on an iPad. She gives a quick glance up amongst the chatter of plastic keys beneath her fingertips.

"How many bags?" she asks in an unfamiliar accent.

"One. One for me. One for him."

"Who is he?"

"My battle buddy," I say jokingly. A term frequently used in Army basic training, but never said in Ranger Battalion due to the likelihood of being slapped for sounding like a boot or "cherry." To our relief, she hands us our boarding passes and takes our bags. Hungry and tired, we wait as our flight is delayed an hour, then two more, and finally departs three hours past schedule. Knowing there's nothing more for us to do but rest for the evening, we embrace the comatose state. My next conscious thought occurs overlooking another continent as the towering mountain peaks welcome Marty and I to Scandinavia.

An easy pass through customs, a new stamp in each of our passports and we step out into a country where neither of us speaks the language or knows a soul. My temperament in this situation settles by the fact it's the third time this year I've had such an experience. Marty is either without angst or hides it well. We have no clue how to get out of the airport. Before leaving the U.S., I took a few screenshots of the surrounding area and know the airport where we landed is isolated from the city of Bergen. Bergen is, in turn, a long mountainous journey to the next large eastern city of Oslo. We talk about trying to hike the distance and essentially just keep walking until our three-week time limit runs out. We hadn't spent much of our initial cash allowance, and in fact, were given even more money along the way from generous and compassionate people. Acquiring a rental car for one day to return in Oslo is an option, until we see the price is more than double what we currently have. We find out an inexpensive bus can drop us off in the Bergen city center. Fortuitously, there's a train station there.

The bus and train stations share a facility in the middle of Bergen. By the time we arrive, no more eastbound trains are leaving. I notice a significant discount for soldiers at the automated electronic ticket station. It doesn't specify whether you have to be a current soldier or even one from this country, so I select this option and inform Marty that we have tickets to Oslo leaving first thing in the morning. With no place to be, we eagerly take to exploring the fairytale landscape of the bustling city disguised as a quaint hillside village.

Soft cool grass comprises the shoreline of the pristine midtown lake. Colossal mountains tower around the city, their reflection perfectly painted upon the lake's liquid crystal surface. The roof tops of colorful homes partially peak out from atop the surrounding hillside forest. Like the lackadaisical movement of the marshmallow clouds above them, drifting white gulls circle freely overhead. Towering trees provide ample shade as we shed our sweaty boots and air out our damp smelly socks in veteran-hobo fashion. Sounds of kids chasing geese and laughing merge with the chirping of birds, completing the soundtrack of the blissful early evening. The sun, not wanting to miss a moment, sits high in the night sky. Further north than either of us have ever been and on the day of the summer solstice, the bright burning ball refuses to give way to the moon for our entire stay in Bergen.

We choke down a meager dinner of military rations provided by our West Point host, Charlie. Marty and I are both anxious to explore the unknown of our newfound surroundings. We drift through the streets and admire the energy of the place, the beauty of the architecture and the lingering fresh smells from the local fish market. The overpriced cost of a cup of coffee from the worldwide chain café is a justifiable expense to be able to recharge our electronic devices and post an update on our recent progress to all the people following our journey. We sit in the coffee shop waiting for night to fall. Hours later it's still light out.

We decide our best bet is to find a secluded area of the park near the train station and try to sleep until we have to catch the train east. Leaving the café, we wander through the winding city streets. Randomly we cross paths with three guys passing around a cheap bottle of vodka. At first it sounds as though one of the men is throwing insults at Marty and me in an unrecognizable language.

"What did you say to me?" I ask aggressively, anticipating a conflict.

"Americans?" He asks with excitement.

"Yeah."

"Ohhh man! That is so great. I am from Finland. This is my friend, he is from here, here in Norway and this fat man we met here. He is a Pol. What are you fellas doing?"

Marty and I explain our trip in as simple of terms as possible.

"Ohh man…Ohh man, so great! You should come have a drink with us, man!"

"OHH YEAH!" his buddy adds.

"I mean, we don't have a lot of money, but would love to hang out with you guys." Marty explains.

"Oh yeah, ohh yeah man. You come with us. We go to the good place, man. Alright!"

What we thought might be an altercation quickly turns into an invitation to experience some Nordic beers. Beers that evolve into shots bought by our newfound friends and Marty and my first experience with the popular little tobacco packets called Snus. Neither Marty nor myself make a habit of indulging in tobacco, so the little pouches stuffed between our gums and lip sets in fast and hard. The synergistic effect with the alcohol amplifies the three drinks in my system threefold with a single dip. Leaving the first bar, the moving cars blur into the background as we stumble through the streets in search of a hidden bar entrance. Drunk and dazed, after some time and the feeling we're being led to a back alley to be clubbed and robbed, our local hosts finally discover the unmarked entrance of the trendy little bar.

The rest of the evening maintains a swift cycle of drinking and dancing. All under the comforting knowledge that none of these people will ever see us again.

Exiting the bar at three o'clock in the morning with a few new female friends is a particularly interesting experience. It's just as light outside as when we entered, and when we originally landed a half a day before.

The promise of the best-fried fish at a local favorite drunk eatery is enough to motivate Marty and myself to continue the sleepless night. The line stretching around the building, however, is demoralizing.

We inadvertently switch hosts from the two Scandinavian guys to two local women in their early twenties. One, who has a kind of "Helga" vibe going on, is not nearly as keen on the idea of the American travelers tagging along to the house party they're en route to. She's clearly agitated I can't pronounce her name. If I'm being honest, I don't remember it. I just give it my best-mumbled guess. I pay much more attention to the piercing on her friend's voluptuous lower lip.

The four of us enter a small, second-story apartment. Immediately a dozen people laughing and listening to music greet us. The friskier of the two who took a particular interest in me, repeatedly touches my arm and giggles wildly. I try not to show my surprise when she walks over to one of the guys in the apartment and kisses him.

"These are my American friends," she mumbles in a semi-coherent slurred state. "This is my boyfriend," she announces.

Going with the flow of the situation I introduce myself, attempting to hide my disappointment. He offers us a drink and we find a spot to sit in the living room. She sits close to me. Very close.

Awkwardly close, knowing now that this is her boyfriend's apartment. Her hand is in my lap as her boyfriend enters the room.

My only thought at this point is: *This will not end well.*

Is she trying to make him jealous? Because I'm not trying to fight this guy and all his friends in his own living room. Of course, between my giant of a friend and I, I'm not concerned with the outcome of the engagement. I'm confident we can easily hold our own against the group of young Europeans in skinny jeans. I just don't want to slap the man in his own home after he mixes me a drink. That will not do well to express our otherwise jovial American tendencies, in our first night abroad.

To my surprise, he doesn't seem to care. I make a move to the other couch as soon as I can without seeming obvious. Later in the conversation, he admits to me that he doesn't care if other guys kiss his girlfriend. I'm not typically the bashful type, however, if he's suggesting I hook up with his girlfriend in front of a group of strangers, well, I'm not drunk enough for that. Earlier in the evening, I made a random comment about jumping in the ocean while I was in town. One of the ladies now hosting us tells me she knows a perfect place. I remind her of her promise and the four of us leave the apartment with no backlash from her boyfriend.

As promised the girls escort Marty and I to a pier and tell us the water below is as deep as it is cold. Without hesitation, I begin to strip down to my underwear and ask, "Is anyone joining me?"

"Ha-ha-ha no, you go alone," the frumpy brute of a girl barks at me.

"Cool with me," I snap back, stepping to the ledge. Leaping through the cool early morning air, the sound of seagulls disappears as the churning sensation of immersion in frigid waters dominates my senses. In an instant, the haze of alcohol and exhaustion cleanses from my accord. By the time I resurface, the world once again radiates with vibrant color and sanguine potential.

Not to be outdone, the adventurous one of the two strips down until there's nothing left but the lacy undergarments which match perfectly her jet black hair; an abrupt contrast to the curves of her milky-white skin. With a slight screech she leaps. An action which brings a smile to my face. The embrace of the moment, the fearless reckless abandon adds to the ongoing human experience, and the disbelief plastered on the face of her prudent friend all mix together to sear the moment deep into the catacombs of my memory.

A short walk away, the girls lead us into a hotel that features a rooftop view promised to be the best we've ever seen. A steep, spiraling staircase ends as the 360-degree view, well above the top of the next highest vantage point in the city, exposes an amalgamation of the harmony of nature and the beauty of Norwegian architecture. We bask in the tranquility of the very moment when the sun would have inched into sight, had it ever bothered to set.

I hand the shivering wet girl my grey hoodie and Marty and I set out for the train station. The maze of now-silent city streets is interrupted only by the sound of Marty and I micturating behind a trash can and laughing in disbelief about the evening we just experienced. A couple of hours later on the train, a large man shakes us awake needing to punch our tickets. When he sees the military discount, he becomes perturbed and we're forced to pay the difference. Following our evening outing and all of the random drinks bought for us, we're both completely drained. We gladly capitulate and hand him the Monopoly-looking money in return for being allowed to slip back into a comatose state. ✺

CHAPTER THIRTEEN

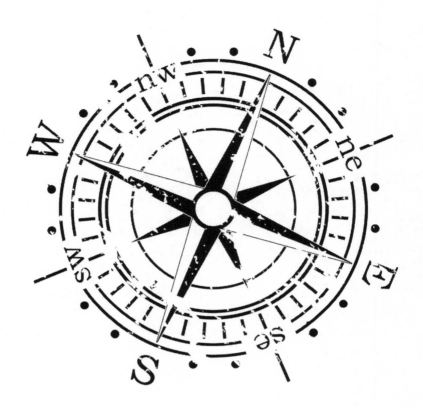

Skål!

"To find yourself, think for yourself."—Socrates

Marty and I both awake as the train finds the end of the line in its easternmost stop. Par for the course, we don't have a plan for how we'll proceed further. To be honest, we're both in a bit of shock that we've made it this far, and still with a little bit of money left. Sitting still now, however, is not an option. We still have close to a week left before our clock expires and we intend to milk every mile out of our bodies.

We discover a source of the Internet at one of the chain burger restaurants in the Oslo train station and begin to search for ways out of the city. Within fifteen minutes I discover a passenger ship headed for Copenhagen, Denmark, at 4 p.m. "Marty, look at this! We already did plane, train, car and foot. Let's get on this boat!"

His eyes light up with excitement. Doing this trip with Marty is easy so far because we both possess an equal amount of desire for new experiences and a genuine belief in the mission we're engaged in.

"The boat leaves in forty minutes and there isn't another one going that way for two more days! Google says the dock is only a few kilometers away."

We quickly abandon all other potential forms of travel and move with purpose toward the marina, dodging and weaving other backpack-clad tourists as we exit the busy train station. All my life I've heard of this magic city and now here I am experiencing it, for the nearly twenty full minutes it takes to run from the train to the boat.

Just minutes before the gates shut and the vessel sets to depart, Marty calmly says something in Norwegian to the beautiful tall blonde behind the counter. Through a beaming smile and blushed cheeks she types for a few seconds on her computer and hands Marty a boarding pass.

"I think we just got hooked up," he whispers to me. I look at the paper in his hand and see that it says "two-person passenger cabin" in bold letters. The price is less than half of what I saw advertised online while sitting in the train station.

"I didn't know you spoke Norwegian, Marty."

"I don't, I really only know like three phrases and that was one of them."

"I don't even care what you said. Whatever it was, well done, amigo!"

We're the final two passengers to cross the little bridge onto the boat. We search back and forth for our room still in disbelief that we exited the train, did a quick Google search for transportation, then found and boarded a boat, all in well under an hour.

Eventually we locate our cabin and laugh like little kids at the bunk bed configuration and small shower. The set up is reminiscent of my grandparents cramped old RV. We each shower and choke down another military-meal-ready-to-eat. The trip to Copenhagen lasts eighteen hours, of which Marty and I sleep for seventeen and a half.

Before falling asleep we send an update on social media stating we're headed to Denmark and would love some help once we arrive. When we wake up there's a message waiting for us from a member of the Royal Danish Army. He tells us that he's happy to pick us up at the marina and show us around the city and even has some work for us, if we're interested. He's followed our travels and knows we're on a mission to help veterans.

Despite our mission being focused on U.S. combat veterans, he's exceptionally eager to help. Even though we've never met, spotting our Danish host is pretty easy. That confident demeanor of a combat veteran, inflated chest and hard eyes, shines like a lighthouse in the night among the crowd of civilians. His smile beams through his thick white beard upon greeting us. As promised, he drives us around the neighborhoods of Copenhagen, giving us a brief history lesson on every street.

The tour concludes at one of the military bases just outside of the city where we're treated to lunch, alongside the Danish soldiers in their dining facility. I don't care how old you get, how far removed you are from your time in service, or whether you're around soldiers from your own nation, walking through the chow line surrounded by camo-clad men and women transports you back. What an experience. What a truly amazing experience to sit shoulder to shoulder with members of another country's army, thousands of miles from anything resembling home, feeling perfectly, comfortably, in your own skin and among your closest of kin.

Following a tour of what I can only describe as a facility that puts most in the U.S. military's collection to shame, we head north to a small fishing village. Our gracious host arranges for Marty and I to spend the evening working at an event, called the midsummer's festival, serving beer and wine.

Aside from setting up a few tents in preparation for the annual event, there isn't much to do before the party begins. We happily accept the invitation to indulge in a cold beer with a few of the local fishermen. A cold beer, in Danish fishing terms apparently means the same as it means in American Army Ranger terms—drink until there are no more beers.

The stream of stories and blue-collar antidotes flow from man to man in a circular fashion. The accent of four different nations contributes to the communal effect of comedic relief. To my surprise, the six-foot-five-inch, three-hundred-pound Scotsman takes little offense to Marty continually referring to him as Irish. Marty and I come close to sharing a case of the frosty suds before it's time to take our place behind the tap at the beer tent we're designated to work in for the evening.

"Feel free to help yourself to as many beers as you want while you work, guys," the director of activities says mistakenly. That sweet, yet terribly naive, woman with the thick Danish accent just opened Pandora's box. Our job is to pour beer and wine and collect the odd-sized shillings in an already half-drunken state.

Luckily, Marty and I receive a crash course in the language, of which, we retain a single, yet highly, useful word. Skål! (Pronounced skawl.) With nearly every libation distributed to our patrons we pour one for ourselves and proceed to toast our newfound friends with the sole word in our foreign vernacular.

After less than an hour, we tell our story a half a dozen times to curious customers and fellow festival workers. One of whom has the idea to write an abbreviated version of what we're trying to accomplish on a piece of cardboard, placing it behind an empty cup at the front of our beer station. The simple act results in a coin tossed in the cup, and then another and another.

Grateful, yet in all honesty quite intoxicated, Marty and I yell, "Skål!" with a slightly more vocal ferocity with each generous tip. The louder we get, the more people feel compelled to donate to our cause. By the end of the evening, the cup is full and we're offered a place to stay with a U.S. Air Force veteran who lives in the area with his wife and newborn.

We thank our host continuously for the food and opportunity to work at such an amazing event, an experience both Marty and I agree is very special and likely not offered to random tourists. We both share how grateful we are to experience a local event that so few foreigners would ever know about, let alone be allowed to partake in.

It doesn't take long for either of us to pass out on our host's living room sofa. As fast as we fall asleep, we awaken to the sublime smell of sizzling bacon and fresh coffee. The lingering effects of the previous evening remind me once again that the repercussion-free days of my early twenties have since given way to the apathetic, pounding morning headaches of my thirties.

The young couple wishes us well, hands us a few of the funny-looking bills and directs us to the local train station, a ten-minute walk away. Even under the weight of our cumbersome packs, Marty and I both stand tall and walk fast. The support of the citizens of yet another nation invigorates our feeling of purpose.

We made the equivalent of three hundred dollars the night before from the sheer generosity of a group of people who don't have to care about us, or what we're trying to accomplish. I understand that the commonplace way of interpreting patriotism is a near-blind love of your own country, and many will argue with me on this point: I believe there can be an extension of such a concept. It isn't the ethnocentric version of patriotism we've become accustomed to. The men who bought our drinks in Bergen, the man willing to go out of his way to pick us up and give us work for the evening and all of the benevolent contributors to our cause believe in the American soldier and firmly stand behind them with the same verve our own citizens' display.

For years, our media has maintained a narrative that our involvement in foreign conflict has created severe disdain and antipathy for the U.S. all over the world. Marty and I begin to discover our own truth, however. A truth that doesn't fall in line with the storyline of global enmity toward our nation's role. At the very least, those we encounter feel a sense of gratitude toward those who volunteer themselves for the sake of others. Whichever it is, Marty and I now have enough money to drive our journey onward.

The short train ride takes us back into the capital city of Copenhagen where we decide to continue south through Germany. Marty, being the intelligent one of the two of us, games our trip and explains to me that the closer we are to the equator, results in a further distance from our start point. Something about the shape of the earth or something like that. So, south it is. We cross into Germany, our fourth country of the trip.

As our new train rockets south, we increasingly become surrounded by water. In an event I never expected to experience in a hundred lifetimes, the train Marty and I are on rolls right onto a boat. I'm not a physics guy. This to me, however, is borderline unexplainable. The fact that I'm still slightly intoxicated from the events of the previous evening makes me initially question the likelihood of what's occurring. Attempting to maintain my composure, I rub my eyes in disbelief. The conductor shouts commands that echo over the train's intercom demanding in German for us to do something. After watching all the other passengers stand up, leave the cars and enter the belly of the ship, I conclude that we're not permitted to stay in place. I'm not inherently claustrophobic, but the zombie-horde master race doing their best imitation of cattle being led to slaughter in the under belly of this boat is enough to make my eye tick.

Short, fast breathing and incessant shifting of a nervous pair of eyes eventually gives way to a childlike excitement as we breach the hull via a pinging-steel staircase in favor of a wide-open deck exposing the totality of our situation. We just rode a train onto a boat, which now takes us across some giant German lake that looks like a scene in a Disney movie.

One new adventure seamlessly merges into the next, extending the blur of continuous human experience. A few packed snacks and another boat nap later, the train realigns with the tracks on the other side of the lake. We opted for the least expensive ticket out of Denmark, which takes us to the Northern city of Hamburg.

Wandering through the train station, we search for a usable Internet connection and exchange our currency for Euros. We discover a bus depot less than a mile away and the tickets for the midnight route south are by far the cheapest way to continue moving. We have just enough time to grab a bottle of water and an apple from a small curbside market before boarding the packed bus headed to Frankfurt.

Marty and I have a mutual friend from our time in the Army who's been stationed there for the last year. It's been a lot longer since I saw Adam than it's been for Marty. Adam and I went through medic school together, as well as the debaucherous evening of my twenty-first birthday in San Antonio, Texas.

He was reprimanded early in his military career and sent to a base in Alaska after a stunt he pulled on Fort Bragg that I'm not entirely comfortable disclosing. After his time in purgatory, he made a triumphant return and eventually was Marty's medic years after I left the military. Adam was always an amazing soldier, and like most amazing soldiers, he was pretty reckless in his early years. His was, however, a unique brand of caution throwing. At twenty years old there was a sort of calculated disregard in him, a restlessness that gave way to decisions that would strike fear in men not easily made afraid. A spark of madness in him best described as unadulterated honesty. Most of those people, who are considered mad, or assholes or jaded in some way, are really just unapologetic truth tellers. Being what the rest of the world expected him to be never seemed to interest him, and for that reason, he always interested me.

Adam picks us up at the bus station in the middle of the city, not a day older than the last time I saw him a decade before. We spend the evening catching up and telling lies about our glory days and drinking too much and forgetting completely that we ever drifted apart.

One of his co-workers spends the evening listening to our bloviating. Something about her captivates me. Perhaps it's the slight shimmer of innocence cautiously hiding in her eyes, hiding behind something heavy and looming, something that comes with being alive. Perhaps it's the shadow of vulnerability that follows her, the result of a recently failed marriage. Whatever that dance is, it effortlessly maintains the softest subtle allure in my mind's imagination.

The next morning after waking on the edge of the couch and indulging in a large breakfast, Adam drives Marty and I a few hours south to the city of Stuttgart. We're offered a ride from there to Zurich, Switzerland, from another foreign soldier following our journey online. In the collective agony associated with overconsumption of German beer, the four of us pile into his car. ✹

CHAPTER FOURTEEN

Europe on a Shoestring

"Buy the ticket, take the ride."—Hunter S. Thompson

In Stuttgart, Adam drops us off in front of a Subway restaurant, says a quick goodbye, and Marty and I begin wandering the streets. Our contact said he has to work until later in the afternoon, so we take advantage of our first opportunity to explore a German city.

The entire town is electrified with the upcoming World Cup game between Germany and the United States. Restaurant workers diligently place flat-screen televisions outside and surround them with folding chairs in anticipation of the growing crowds of spectators. The alleyway streets begin to fill with waves of locals, adorned with patriotic face paint, eager to cheer on their nation's team. There are four, maybe five Americans in sight. Their overstated attire dripping with red, white and blue makes the away fans a dead giveaway.

A short time after the start of the match, Dani joins us. We're already posted up at one of the small, but packed sidewalk bars watching the game. Dani has been an active member of the German Army for several years. His short, red beard hides his young face. He carries himself with the quiet confidence of a soldier. We sit watching the match together for close to an hour.

It would not be our day. The United States' loss is honestly the better outcome for Marty and I. Had we won, I'm not entirely sure I would have resisted the urge to chant U.S.A., U.S.A. at the top of my lungs, potentially resulting in a great deal of physical harm being brought to each of us. As Marty and I climb into Dani's car, the energy of the spectators begins to amplify intensely. These German sports fans quickly graduate to fanatics, waving enormous flags and rocking massive charter busses back and forth. The traffic is at a complete standstill as fans display their enthusiasm by flooding the streets.

"This is nuts!" Marty exclaims, recording everything with a small handheld camera we're using to document our trip.

"Yeah, that's how it is. Beating America is a big deal," Dani explains in his thick German accent.

"I guess that makes it two to one, yeah?" I add sarcastically.

Dani tries to interject, "This is the only time the two countries have faced each other."

"You sure about that?" I add. Marty knows what I'm getting at and just shakes his head, a fact that does little to deter me from teasing our host a little more.

"We won the two times that it mattered, though," I finish, laughing. Tact was never one of my stronger qualities. Dani is a good sport about the joke. Through the laughter my mind wanders off and into the thought that had this been seventy-one years before, we wouldn't be making jokes with each other. Marty and I being soldiers in the U.S. Army would be trying to kill Dani and he'd be trying to do the same to us, right here in this very countryside we're driving through. He is so similar to us. He laughs at the same jokes, reads the same books and has experienced the same tribulations, being a young veteran of a foreign war.

On his wrist Dani wears a black metallic bracelet honoring a fallen soldier from the unit Marty and I served in. It is heavily worn, suggesting it's seldom removed from his wrist. A subtle, yet significant, testament of the comradery he feels with American soldiers and the respect he has for their sacrifices.

Marty and I take full advantage of the opportunity to inquire about life in the German Army. We learn how much more progressively they handle post-traumatic stress related to combat than our country does. He tells us about meeting veterans of World War II. Men who fought under the Nazi flag. The gravity of such a thing is not lost on either of us.

Sometime after midnight we roll through the border and into Zurich. Without a plan, Dani drops us off at the train station. Before he leaves he hands me a patch he carried with him in Afghanistan. It was in memory of Ben Kopp, a U.S. Army Ranger who sacrificed himself to save his fellow Rangers, one of whom being a man I was formerly a medic for. With a simple gesture, the world shrinks to a tiny neighborhood and illuminates the intertwining essence of the human connection, now solidified in my heart. "I want you to have this, to carry it with you on your journey. I think that he would like that."

I didn't know Ben personally. We served at the same time in the same small unit, yet never met. Taken aback by the gesture, I accept with gratitude. Dani has a long drive back to the military post where he's stationed, paired with an early morning formation tomorrow. I sign a copy of my first book for my new friend. With a big hug we part ways, knowing we've made a friend for life.

It's well past midnight and the train station is closed for the evening. Patrolling guards keep vagrants like us from sleeping on any of the benches. Marty and I spend the better part of an hour seeking a place to flop for what's left of the evening. Each spot out of the way enough to get a little sleep is already occupied by a fellow hobo.

Eventually, after ascending halfway up a long concrete staircase overlooking the train station, we locate a couple of bushes.

"That's it! Right there, the Ritz!" I call out to Marty as I quickly begin to loosen the straps of my bulky pack. I pull out the thin sleeping bag and proceed to tuck myself into the bush. I hardly notice the cold night air permeating the light cover and attacking my skin. I fall asleep instantly.

In the early glow of first light I see Marty perched on one of the steps chewing on a cheek full of sunflower seeds. "Did you sleep?" I ask.

"No. I've been watching these hookers pick guys up and take them into that apartment building. That one there has been busy. That's her third guy tonight."

I chuckle at my friend's intrigue and brush the dirt and leaves from my clothes. We make our way down to the bus station and find an inexpensive ticket into Milan, Italy. What I'm sure is one of the more scenic rides anywhere in the world is traded for the sight of the inside of my eyelids. I fall fast asleep to the sound of the now-routine comfort of a rumbling train car.

Italy is the sixth country we trek into this week. A dozen old men sit and fuel their vibrant storytelling with bottomless espresso drinks at an aromatic café across from the train station. We are in Milan just long enough to arrange a ride to Vicenza, a couple of hours east. Two former professional cyclists give us a hitch, dropping us off at one of the off-ramps on the outskirts of the city. The driver allows us the use of his phone to set up a ride from an old Army buddy, now stationed in Italy. Once they drop us off, however, we no longer have a way to communicate with my contact. For hours we sit in the grass by the side of road, trapped between the freeway to our north and a vast amount of nothing to our south.

Well after dark, we decide our ride won't be coming. We have to make something happen on our own. We seem to be several miles from the actual town, but understand a populated area is our best chance to maintain momentum. Navigating the major freeway between the town and us will be a little bit of an issue, however.

The police stop us on our first attempt. We rethink our strategy. Looking highly suspicious, we try to position ourselves to play frogger across a major freeway.

I begin laughing hysterically as we crouch and crawl and bound our way over a series of concrete barricades and a bridge clearly not intended for foot traffic. We illegally dart across one section of highway, and then another, overstuffed backpacks swaying in the warm summer breeze. The moment liberates me. A jovial return to juvenile delinquency.

Here we are in a country where neither of us has ever been, violating a series of laws late into the evening, like a couple of restless kids on summer vacation. I feel like an overgrown child in the middle of a game of hide-and-seek with law enforcement. These are the moments that make a lifetime.

We walk over eight miles to the town, which is now turned off for the evening. One restaurant, illuminated by strands of white patio lights, remains open.

"Fuck it, I don't even care how much it costs. I'm getting some pizza," Marty proclaims unprovoked, charging toward the establishment. Given our budget, it seems like a frivolous, yet warranted, purchase.

We've been so cautious with our spending knowing we need every Euro to get as far as possible. We have a mission, a very important mission, but we also refuse to pass on a new life experience. Since the ice cream cone in Colorado, this pizza in Italy is the first item we pay to indulge in for ourselves.

After we leave the restaurant, the number of prostitutes on the streets is staggering. Progressively as we move further from the nice part of town and closer to the bus station, the general condition of the young women dissipates until they're no longer young and, in some cases, not even women.

At first, the onslaught of propositions entertains me. However, by the time the two burly dress-wearing, Adam's apple having, tooth-missing hookers grab at my arm and insist I pay them for sex, I begin to get a little concerned. It becomes necessary to remind myself that Marty and I are both battle-hardened former special operation soldiers and are perfectly capable of handling the grabby streetwalkers. Even still, I'm a little uneasy.

Eventually, after a few wrong turns and some second-guessing, we find the train and bus station. We're unsurprised to see it's closed for the evening. The park across the street has signs banning anyone from sleeping in the area, a warning Marty and I choose to completely ignore as we post up under a tree and drift asleep. For the second night in a row I immediately pass out and Marty stays awake, watching the surrounding area like a gargoyle.

The morning comes too soon. We're forced to move before the daylight gives away our relatively unhidden location. Dragging ourselves back into the train station, we decide Venice is a natural choice. It's a short distance away and a city that long intrigued us both. Arriving there, our hope is to find a boat to take us across the Adriatic Sea and into Croatia. This proves to be more of a challenge than either of us anticipated.

We'd maintained such success fluidly and effortlessly moving from city to city that our experience in Venice becomes instantly frustrating. We can't find a boat, we're running out of time and money, and we don't even have the option to walk further east, due to the fact that water completely surrounds the city.

During my travels I've been fortunate enough to explore a lot of cities throughout the world and Venice is truly the most unique, a fact that helps to settle the anxiety stemming from the feeling we've made an extensive tactical mistake by coming here. First of all, there isn't a single car in the entire city, so hitchhiking is out of the question.Waterways provide routes of transportation via small boats. The entire place feels like a movie.

A short conversation with two English travellers gives Marty and I the opportunity to tell our story, one more time. Compelled by our tale, the two ladies in their mid-twenties give us twenty euros to help us out. The way the elderly couple gave us money for food without us asking in the McDonald's so many miles ago, these two offer assistance without prompting. In a big way, it saves us.

We have enough money now for two train tickets to the next closest city to the east. With a few hours to kill, we set out to explore the city, getting lost in the never-ending twisting back alleys and maze-like corridors.

Perhaps it's the heat of the mid-summer day, or the residual effect of intermittent sleep, or the arduous weight of my pack, but navigating the otherwise breathtaking city becomes more chore than treat. Voracious hordes of photo-ravenous sightseers along with multitudinous rows of trinket hucksters looking to exploit them, embezzle any authenticity from the experience. A tourist trap is a tourist trap, despite the splendor of its uniquity.

On the morning of our final day, we rumble into the city of Trieste, the lagging exhaustion drapes over our shoulders. Pulling together the last few coins between the two of us, we have just enough for a slice of heat lamp, train station pizza. We fill our water bottles from the bathroom sink and discuss our next move. The Slovenian border looks so close on the digital map on my iPad.

"You up for a little hike, Leo?" Marty asks suggestively. If we can make it before midnight, it will mark the seventh country of our trip, which started three weeks ago with a hundred dollars and a backpack. He knows the answer before he asks.

We take advantage of the train station café's WiFi, spending a half an hour studying the maps. It appears there's one major throughway that acts as an artery from the larger city of Trieste to the rural western portion of Slovenia. It seems simple enough, find the major road and follow it east.

We set out with verve. The compounding effects of so many nights with inadequate sleep and so many missed meals, however, quickly become a noticeable factor. Raw blistered feet make each step more uncomfortable than the previous.

The midday summer heat crushes us with callous disregard. The road east is uphill, taking us from sea level to over 1,200 feet through the course of just a couple of miles.

Inner thighs are chafed raw and bleeding by the time we run out of water. All the while, I still carry, literally everything I own in the world on my back. A quantity of possessions that previously made me feel like a minimalist, however, I begin to reassess my need for seventy pounds of anything more and more with each mile.

All of our mapping devices are out of power, leaving us to guess which road to take. We rely entirely on instinct now. Uncertainty of direction adds to the draining effects of the situation. An amalgamation of stubborn pride, grit, and fear of looking weak in front of one another drudgingly drives our two-man convoy forward.

Like a carrot from the heavens, dangled in front of us to prompt motivation, a scintillating myriad color falls gently against the backdrop of a placid sea in what can only be described as the most incredible sunset I've ever witnessed. Once again, we halt the mission in favor of soaking up serenity. All our superficial discomforts dissipate and fade along with the daylight. Through the darkness we move in the direction we assume is east. Every mile is another dollar for our fellow veterans in need, a fact that keeps us moving.

We each have a single M.R.E. left. Just after sundown, we decide that if we're going to walk until midnight we need calories. Without water, we choke down the unpalatable contents of the brown plastic package. This is the first meal of our trip spent in silence.

Each of us has gone to that place, that place we knew as soldiers. That silent resolve of a quiet professional, tattered, yet never broken. Years removed from our physical prime, yet as mentally focused as ever. Rigidly aware that no hard time, no suffering, no adversity can outlast our accord. We were soldiers, and always will be.

Joints creak and pop as we stand to continue our movement. My mind exudes a temperate resilience, my knees, however, tell another story. The darkness fully settles in, bringing with it the damp chill night air. Our sweat-soaked clothes, just an hour ago uncomfortably sweltering, now chill us to our core. With bloody feet we march.

The desolate eerie dirt road we walk is likely tranquil in the daylight, however, we have no idea where we are, or if we're even traveling in the right direction. We have no idea what time it is, or how far we've actually gone.

I clutch a knife in my dominate hand as the limited stream of illumination bounces erratically from Marty and my headlamps, guiding the way to nowhere. The wind howls through the indistinguishable trees. I feel the eyes of a dozen creatures following my every step.

"Do you think there are any bears out here, Marty?"

"Hmm, I don't think so. Maybe werewolves, but probably not any bears."

As Marty finishes his response, an intense and violent rustle in the bushes to my right stimulates my heart to surge, preparing my body with the necessary amount of blood for the eventual need to run. Sweat accumulates between the rigid contours of the knife handle and the skin of my palm. *Ahh, my old friend, adrenaline.*

Without discussion or individual intention, we both significantly increase our cadence. A dim light appears in the distance. A slight beacon of hope in an otherwise tenebrous evening. Moving slowly into a small town, the chime of church bells ring out a dozen crisp tones. The sound of midnight welcomes us to the town of Lipica, Sezana, a village in Slovenia.

With no crowd to welcome us, in as anticlimactic moment imaginable, we cross the arbitrary finish line we set for ourselves. Our seventh country this week and some eight thousand miles from that Denver train yard. As unceremonious as it began, our experience ends. Too tired for any meaningful reflection, we stumble toward the small inn located in the center of town.

Our arrival surprises the little old innkeeper. He shows concern for the obvious labored way Marty and I limp in, both attempting to find the one spot on our feet that isn't bleeding to set gently on the ground.

No longer restricted by our original budget, we're free to indulge in a couple of beds, complete with pillow and sheets. The place might be a complete dive for all we know. It feels like a palace. The ninety euros we pay for the room is more money than we started with. It makes me feel sick to some degree. My perception on the value of certain items compared to their relative cost has since shifted drastically.

My desire for comfort has now given way to the need for movement. A shift that will come to plague me in the days and weeks to come. Such rapid movement sparks a long, subdued flame in me; one that will burn to ash the pleasures of experience which I spent so many stagnant years longing for. ✦

CHAPTER FIFTEEN

An Uncomfortable Solitude

"Our doubts are traitors, and make us lose the good we oft might win, by fearing to attempt."—William Shakespeare

Breakfast in Austria, lunch in Budapest, a quick snack in Slovakia, then dinner in Prague. Four countries today. Tomorrow my flight leaves for Moscow, then off to Bangkok. No high profile business trip accelerates my movement. Like a runaway train, I slam myself into travel hyperspeed. As if I can see my own expiration date and have to check as many boxes as possible before time runs out. Marty has already returned to the United States to his pregnant wife with the pride of a mission successfully accomplished. We raised close to thirty thousand dollars for the veteran charity, GallantFew. We conducted over a dozen television and radio interviews bringing attention to the cause and spoke with countless people, citizen and soldier alike, on the perils of returning from war without direction. Where does that leave me though? A month ago I had no intention of being in Europe and now here I am and on my own.

The places to go and sights to see on this continent are as near infinite as the stars above it. Perhaps that's why I feel so tiny, so alone. Marty and I created an effective pattern of quickly saying goodbye to each passing host, yet always maintaining one another's company. In a similar fashion, when it was time for him to return to the States, he pressed on as though still on our mission. I did the same, just in the opposite direction. A stoic separation appropriate for two aging soldiers, neither investing emotional coin on departing from a good friend. Even after all we accomplished, we overcame, and grew with one another, the most fitting farewell confined to, "I'll see you when I see you."

Now for the first time, I'm completely unaccompanied and attempting to digest the magnitude of all that's transpired. I've never experienced a more painful solitude amidst such a dense population. A grey haze blankets even the most luminous human experience when traversed alone.

I spend my final night in Europe watching the U.S. lose another World Cup match, surrounded by different groups of tourist travelers in the city of Prague. The long walk back to my hotel room is protracted by my lack of bearing. I'm lost.

Alone. Adrift. Among a sea of faces and cackling conversations. Searching for a road that leads home. Seeking solace in familiarity, but finding none. The agony of this evolution continues. Departure from comfort is simply the seed. Transcendence into a towering oak of internal faith begins with that seed. What great man has ever been, who was not first self-reliant? What person ever came to that state without first experiencing the anguish of isolation?

My time in Moscow is as short as my experience in Prague. Buildings and blank faces. Void of all emotion when viewed through the lens of desolation. Before I know it, I'm on a plane headed for Thailand. My only thought when taking my seat is how ready I am for a long nap. The boisterous, stereotypical Russian sitting to my right has something else in mind, however. It's apparent to me he has not interacted much with people from the United States. He's amused by the opportunity to practice his limited English vernacular. Most of which he directs toward the flight attendant in a barrage of misogynistic requests for free beverages.

In the thickest Russian accent I've ever heard, "Aaah, pretty lady, bring me Coca-Cola." He repeats this phrase every time the trim young blonde walks by, while aggressively nudging me in the ribs with his elbow. By the time we land, he's proclaimed almost every advance in technology over the past two decades has come from the ingenuity of brilliant Russian scientists and consumed enough of the sugary libation to wire a class of preschoolers for a month.

I conducted little research or planning before arriving in Bangkok. The feeling of entering a foreign country without a plan, once again, stimulates a greater sense of adventure. I know I want to visit the large island of Phuket, but decide to figure out the details as I go. Learning the way the little chip for the inner city rail system confuses me at first, but I figure it out quickly. Navigating to the larger national train station is fluid enough and not terribly unlike most of the other places I've recently been.

The sheer number of people cramming to capacity the tiny cars is a bit overwhelming, however. Two to three times the number of people occupy the same public transit space than even the most crowded subway I'd traveled in New York City. Despite being packed, I witness young men consistently giving up their seats to any elderly passengers who board.

The hot sticky air sags heavy in the downtown train depot, making the four-hour wait for the next train to Phuket unbearable. Making my way to the public bathroom, I'm overcome by a blitzkrieg of noxious pungent shit particles bombarding my nares. A pruned human being, clearly immune to the toxic fecal cloud, sits at the entrance collecting coins. *I have to pay to go in there?* Knowing that my only other option is to aimlessly wander the crowded streets in search of a latrine, I pay the five Baht and step forth into the dragon's lair.

Like the city train, the washroom facilities are crowded well beyond capacity. Lined like soldiers, shoulder to shoulder, the men stand shirtless at the dinghy metallic wash basin, bathing. I make every effort not to stare. Instead, I look to the stall doors to my right. Each one seemingly occupied. Standing in place waiting, men shuffle past me, bumping and jockeying for a position at the sink. I pounce at the first available toilet, not wanting to breathe anymore of the vile, viscous environment for a moment longer than necessary.

Decades of grime stain the tiles like the teeth of a longtime coffee addict. A small trash can sits tucked in the corner. A nozzle not unlike the one I used to do the dishes with as a kid, is attached to a three-foot hose, connected to the wall. What I don't see is toilet paper. In fact, there isn't even a place to hold a roll of the staple sanitary product. The ever-building abdominal pressure slows my uptake of the situation. I believe the intention is to grab that formerly white, now camouflaged, nozzle and use it to clean myself post defecation.

The trash can, however, suggests that paper is disposed of on a regular enough basis to warrant its presence. Perhaps it's just this stall lacking the necessary white commodity. Once again, I wait for another stall to open. Nothing. Another minute, and the situation becomes increasingly dire. I may pass out soon. Waiting for the third stall to become available, I have a short flashback to the gas chamber in basic training where new troops are exposed to CS gas and made to recite their name, rank and social security number.

The onslaught is too much to handle, I'm about to pass out. *Please, please don't let me pass out and fall onto this floor. My immune system isn't built for that level of bacteria.* Just before I black out from the smell, I notice the little old lady, or man who collects the toll at the front door, also sells single sheets of toilet paper. I dig into my right pocket and pay for a fistful of the white gold. *What a beautiful racket*, I think to myself, as I leave the single most feculent environment I've ever willingly entered.

I wander out into the overcrowded city streets. A tidal wave of shouting men solicit me for a ride on their three-wheeled rickshaw scooters called *Tuk-tuks*. Everything is overcrowded causing a perpetual feeling of claustrophobia. The heat wears me down. One Tuk-tuk driver, who speaks decent English, offers to show me the sights for a reasonable price. For some reason, I have no interest in seeing the typical landmarks where he's accustomed to taking tourists. None of my moving cultural experiences so far resulted from waiting in line to take a picture of a building. In fact, I don't take a single photo during my tour of the vast bustling city. Instead, I ask the driver to take me to where he likes to eat lunch.

The language barrier proves problematic. Either that, or he knows he won't receive a kickback for taking me to a hole-in-the-wall eatery. Instead, we go to another tourist hotspot, and another, each time I refuse to even leave the tiny cart. Perhaps this makes me appear as an unpleasable foreign customer. The reality is my desire is for true experience, not a photo to wave in people's faces on social media, proclaiming, "Look at me, look at the places I'm going and you're not, you should feel jealous."

Frustrated, hot, and hungry, he drops me off back at the train station, having never indulged in any of the exquisite culinary delights which Bangkok may or may not offer.

I look forward to the bed in the cabin upgrade I paid for. So much so that I board the train nearly a half an hour before it's set to depart. For those unfamiliar with train travel, one of the simple pleasures no longer shared with air travel is you can literally board a minute before departure. What a liberating mode of transportation to allow its patrons the freedom, bag in hand, knife in pocket, ticket recently purchased for the same price it was a month ago, to hop aboard and maintain migration.

As I board, I notice the bunk is above my seat. I seem to be the first one on the train. The weight of my eyelids becomes increasingly difficult to manage. Just as I begin to succumb to the jet lag, two girls in their mid-twenties sit down across the aisle from me. A sharply dressed guy their same age, who sits down in the seat directly across from mine, accompanies them. He introduces himself as "Adam" in a heavy English accent. In the middle of his thin face sits two inquisitive eyes, open and examining his surroundings. I return the pleasantry and introduce myself. He recognizes I'm an American and we begin to chat. A woman selling beer walks by as the train begins to depart. By now, Adam and I are well into our conversation about traveling. We share an enthusiasm for new places and each buys a 32-ounce beer from the steward.

As they have a habit of doing, one large beer multiplies into another and another, and our conversation evolves from politics to philosophy, the disturbing excess most people in each of our respective countries take for granted, and the name of the guy who invented the thing at the end of the shoelace.

Two male passengers in their early twenties boisterously interrupt our bilateral inquiry. The louder of the two is built like a rugby player, speaks with a heavy Irish accent and is clearly under the influence of large amounts of drugs and alcohol. The other, a slightly smaller American, sports a similar slur and wobble. Bored out of their minds, they walk up and down the aisleway of each of the cars. Seeing that Adam and I are of a similar age and drinking, they invite themselves to sit with us.

The comedic relief is welcome as the two divulge their excessive recreational consumption of Xanax before boarding the train. Awake for three days and partying in the capital, they decided to get on a random train. The two met in a whorehouse in Bangkok while hammered and have been together since.

"You guys like scotch?" the delirious American asks Adam and I. "I got a bottle of twelve-year-old Black Label, if you want to share it." We gladly accept the offer and Tweedle Dee and Tweedle Dumb excuse themselves to go locate their possessions.

"Unfucking real, eh?" Adam says shaking his head laughing as the two stumble off.

They return twenty minutes later with bottle in hand and stupid glassed-over looks plastered on their faces. Without prompting, the young Irishmen pulls his phone from his pocket and grins as he proudly shows us a picture his friend just captured of him hanging from the back of the train. Dick in the wind. Completely naked. A group of onlookers in the background.

"What. The. Fuck?" I don't even know how else to respond. I want to ask, "What in the hell would compel a person to hang naked from the back of a moving train, heavily intoxicated, while his buddy takes pictures?" Abruptly, a flash image of my early twenties enters my memory and it seems less odd.

"Come on, you guys gotta come try this!"

"No, no that is not something that I feel like I just have to try," Adam replies, soberly. "That actually looks like a bloody-awful, fucking idea."

The two just laugh hysterically, setting down the unopened bottle of Johnnie Walker and mumble something about "one more time." Taking them up on the offer to partake in their scotch, Adam and I down close to half the bottle. Another half an hour passes before the two return.

This time they each pull out their phones and proceed to show a series of photos featuring both of them hanging off the side of the train, cigarette in mouth, naked as the day they were born, high fiving each other. I can't help but think about the inevitable dick trauma inflicted, if they lost their grip. Adam's concern seems more relevant, however.

"If you're both hanging off the side of the train, who the fuck took the pictures?"

"Huh?"

"Who took the pictures of the two of you?" Adam inquiries for the second time, as the little Thai lady who sells beers walks by a fourth time. This time she begins laughing uncontrollably at the two eccentric passengers. The look on her face answers Adam's question.

Once more the two invite themselves to sit in our already-cramped quarters, passing out almost immediately. Adam and I conclude the only logical thing to do is to finish the entire bottle of scotch before retiring for the evening. We each manage a little under an hour of sleep before the train halts at our stop.

We exit the train leaving the now-drooling duo in their comatose state. The idea of the shock they're in for when they wake up completely unaware of where they are or how they got there sends me into a fit of laughter.

The repercussions of a half a bottle of booze and another sleepless night come calling on the four-hour bus ride from the train station to Phuket. The filthy, choking heat of the unairconditioned bus rolling through the jungle robs me of the last remaining moisture in my body. My tongue swells as another wretched hangover sets in.

A swift kick to the gut starts my day. Not metaphorically speaking, an actual kick to the abdomen wakes me up. It's just past seven in the morning and I'm already drowning in my own sweat. A twenty-year-old, hundred-and-twenty pound Muay Thai fighter "warms me up" with a few snapping front kicks to my midsection.

"Ooiii!" he shouts, celebrating each time he connects.

The rhythmic snap of a jump rope grazing the sweat-stained mats in the background, fuses with the concussive force of shin and elbow skin slapping the various hanging punching bags all around me. It's my third consecutive day of legitimate Muay Thai instruction, meaning it's my third consecutive day without a drink. I set the intention to clear my mind and body of all toxins while attempting to absorb the cultural tranquility of Thailand.

Tranquility can often come at a price, however. Today that price is going ten rounds with a professional who has over a hundred fights to his credit. I made the mistake of telling the lead instructor I have previous experience in kickboxing, so I'm tossed to the whims of the advanced-level fighters. A trial by cultural fire. Each day over the next five weeks I bathe in the tumultuous ruckus and resulting serenity that is the national sport of Muay Thai.

After a little over a week, my instructors invite me to attend one of their sanctioned fights in a nearby town. I'm told to meet them at the gym and ride with them to the venue. I'm amazed by how relaxed the two men are on the twenty-minute drive. We all sit in the back of a pickup truck and they laugh and joke like we're headed to a party. In less than two hours they'll each co-headline a fight in front of a thousand people. They don't display the nervousness I experienced each time I headed to compete in a fight in my early twenties. They have no apprehension or thought of it. This combat is routine, a way of life. Each of my two coaches fighting tonight have roughly one-hundred-and-twenty professional fights and neither is over the age of twenty three. They both competed for the first time at the age of twelve and regularly fight once a month, earning a couple thousand Baht each time (roughly $55 U.S. dollars). Not enough to live on, but if you add what they make coaching, they can support themselves by training and fighting alone.

For around thirty dollars I secure a ringside seat. Fifteen fights are on tonight's card and I'm surprised to see they start off with a junior's division. The youngest of the fighters being twelve years old. In the corner of the muggy indoor stadium, a live band plays traditional Thai music as the young men make their way to the ring, wearing the customary robe and head dressing. Prior to bowing to one another, each pay respect to the ring, the audience, and the judges in a ceremonial dance. The level of respect displayed by these pre-teens is greater than I've ever witnessed at any level of sports in the United States.

The high-pitched chime of the fight bell sets in motion a two-way, typhonic assault of elbows, knees, feet and fists. Without a single protective pad between them, these two young warriors engage in round after round of cataclysmic fury and unwavering determination. Neither of the two are tall enough to see over the top rope, yet fight with a higher degree of technical merit and difficulty than any opponent I'd ever personally faced in the United States. When their fight concludes, each pays much-deserved respect to the other and takes no part in any boastful action. This theme continues through each of the subsequent fights.

Partway through the evening, I notice I'm one of only a few white people in attendance. This particular venue is a local establishment. Men shake money at one another, betting on their favorite fighters and collectively embrace the victory of a successful strike. This is in direct contrast to the sounds heard in American fighting arenas, where the crowd collectively groans in sympathetic agony for the person receiving the blow. Here the audience vocally celebrates the athletes making the successful impact.

Despite being in what's widely considered a more tourist-dense part of the country, I find relaxing easy here. The locals are more than hospitable and the rolling mountainous jungle terrain perfectly backdrops the song of crystal clear waves pressing effortlessly onto the golden sand upon my feet. I forego the temptations of all the night has to offer, all that it has to take from me, in favor of the early morning sun cresting from just behind the distant statue of Buddha, set high on a hill. Exploration becomes my new vice as I spend my afternoons dodging carnivorous cars on the rented red rocket scooter. At a cost of three dollars a day, the mode of transportation is as affordable as it is hair-raisingly dangerous.

I make it my goal to eat at a different establishment for every meal. Four times a day for over a month means finding over a hundred different eateries. That means exploring every nook and cranny of the large island. The seafood and noodle dishes are without rival in most places I find. A bottle of Chang mineral water and large meal is seldom more than four dollars and contains none of the typical plastic ingredients found in American fast food.

One fateful evening, however, my experience with some back-alley Pad Thai nearly turns deadly as my internal contents violently exit my body in projectile fashion from orifice multiple. One and only one good thing comes from the inability to get out of bed for nearly three full days, and that's watching a pirated disc of the first three seasons of *Game of Thrones* from the fetal position.

Before leaving Thailand, I find a tattoo artist and add the five-inch logo to my leg from the company that donated to Marty and my campaign. The new ink is the sole souvenir I take with me as my journey continues across another ocean, miles above the sea, to another continent furthering the quest to escape, fly higher, and locate a something which I cannot yet identify. ✸

CHAPTER SIXTEEN

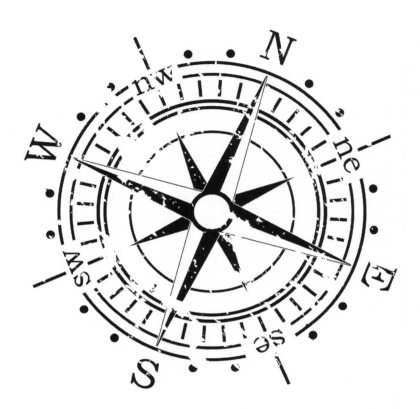

Getting Back Up, Down Under

*"Happiness is the meaning and purpose of life,
the whole aim and end of human existence."*—Aristotle

Movement has become my drug. The euphoric rush passes through my veins as I exit another train station. Surrounded on all sides by concrete giants in the heart of a brand new city. Once again strangers rush by, confident in their destination and exactly how to get there. As much as I try to fit in, the look of bewilderment plastered on my face and the sixty-pound bag on my back is a dead giveaway. Step one, find a staging place for old red, then a decent meal. Less than one hour earlier I landed in Sydney, Australia without a clue as to where I'll go from the airport. A quick Google search displays an intercity train that drops off at Sydney's Central Station, which doesn't appear to be too far from about a dozen hostels and, more importantly, the Sydney Opera House. I can't say why I've always wanted to see the Opera House. It's actually a bit strange. Most iconic man-made structures are of little-to-no interest to me, yet for some reason, I've always felt compelled to see this one.

Dodging a series of fit-looking Aussies out for a run, I push uphill toward the closest hostel. Within five minutes of Central Station is a place called Home Hostel. For twenty-five dollars I secure a bed for the evening in a room with five other travelers—my first experience in a six-person hostel room. After years in the military, sharing a single room with multiple bunk beds and lockers with strangers didn't seem terribly concerning. These gentlemen, however, did not maintain the same standard of cleanliness, which I became accustomed to in the Army. Their shit is everywhere. There's only a single top bunk available in the room I'm assigned to.

It's apparent that at thirty-one years of age, I'm senior to everyone else in the room by around a decade. Most people who travel like this seem to get it out of their system in their early twenties. Having the responsibility of fighting two wars during that period of my life, this is my opportunity to explore the hostel life. Being a decade removed from your so-called peers isn't of much concern when you're the older one. However, the look displayed on the faces of the younger occupants always hints of, "What are you doing here, grandpa?"

I ask about the best local food spots and any must-see attractions in the area. Being back in a country of fellow English speakers is a relief and makes communication much easier. Despite the fact that most people in many countries know enough English to get through a basic conversation, I couldn't help but feel rude for making them speak my language in their country. Most people don't seem to mind, but as a visitor, it tends to make me feel disrespectful to not be fluent.

The man behind the desk at the hostel welcomes me and informs me that the Sydney Opera House is a nice twenty-minute walk through the park. The slow stroll to the opera house is incredible. Once again I have no idea what's around each corner. It's all new, every step an adventure. Old fountains and statues line the way. Basking in the warmth of the sunny day, people lounge in the fresh-cut grass reading while others toss a ball. The city reminds me of Denver. Groups in athletic gear who appear to have just finished a run gather at a busy sidewalk café enjoying an afternoon beer, joking and laughing collectively. Half a world away from where I was born, there's no doubt in my mind that I could sit down with that group and feel completely at home. The instant feeling of commonality is a welcomed change from my feelings of relative disconnect while in Asia.

Within minutes I spot the tip of the famous white structure I'm searching for. It peeks out between two tall buildings with the sun cast on it in perfect symmetry. I feel like a little kid seeing the top part of a roller coaster from the family minivan while approaching the amusement park for the first time. The cadence of my step increases as I move closer and closer. My heart rate begins to increase slightly and I'm not even sure why. Over the past few months, I've seen dozens of iconic structures, yet for some reason this one exhilarates me. A few more steps and the expressive shape takes form in front of me, peeking out from behind another building and showcasing its unique beauty for first time. A grin stretches my face to capacity. My eyes light up.

This is it. This is why I travel. Millions of people had cast gaze on this magnificent edifice long before my arrival. Millions more will experience its splendor after I depart, but in this moment, I discover it myself. Alone, I brought myself to this moment, this present reality. I've always wanted to see this arbitrary pile of concrete, drawn to it by some inexplicable force.

It's just a thing, but so are all things. It's just a place, but so are all places. The difference is, I made it happen. I created my destiny. Too often I'd heard, "I wish I could go there," or "I wish I could travel." The only person who ever kept me from this moment was me. I could have stood on those steps years ago, but I wasn't ready. I thought there needed to be a perfect time or I had to find someone to accompany me. On the steps of the opera house, I unpeel the layers of lies I laid down.

Surrounded by hundreds of people, yet completely alone, the collective entirety of my senses encapsulates this moment. It's mine and forever will be. A moment where the fear of solitude leaves me. A moment where I understand fully that my movement, my destiny, my life is entirely mine to live and to dictate and to mold however I see fit. This is a moment singing of limitless possibilities. Fear of being alone vanquished by the solace of a reborn faith in my ability to stand on my own, to walk in silent stride and absorb all the beauty and joy of life without necessity of reciprocation.

The rumbling of my empty stomach disrupts the tranquility of the moment. It's nearly three o'clock in the afternoon and I haven't eaten anything since last night. The walk back toward the hostel becomes more of a mission for sustenance than a sightseeing venture. Walking past a small café I poke my head in to see what's on the menu. The warm welcome from the attractive brunette behind the counter is enough of a reason to choose this establishment.

I try to remain calm as the small bottle of juice and petite chicken wrap ring up for more than three times the cost of the most decadent meal I purchased while in Thailand. I was warned that Australia is expensive, still I'm taken aback. I produce a funny-looking yellow bill from my pocket and receive a purple, a red and a blue bill in return. The picture of the cowboy riding a horse on one note distracts me from the cost of the meal.

Walking back through the park I notice a reflective pool and old monument, resembling the Lincoln Memorial in Washington, D.C. on a smaller scale. In front of the pond three skateboarders attempt to outdo one another with various tricks.

It seems like the perfect place to sit and enjoy my late lunch. I laugh at the large white sign with bold red letters banning skateboarding in this area.

"Defiance is the heart of liberty," according to Thoreau. These guys exemplify such a belief. The attitude is refreshing. There was, to me, an unfamiliar obedient tone echoed in the actions of the people in Thailand. The United States was born of rebellion. Much has changed since becoming an independent and sovereign nation over two hundred years ago, but one thing remains constant: We don't like being told what to do. So much so, I've seen people speak out against a law they don't even disagree with on the simple premise that they should not be infringed upon. The guys doing kick flips on the steps of that monument would fit right in back home.

As I choke down the dry tortilla-wrapped chicken, I swear I'm in a park back home as I observe the diverse groups of people passing by. It doesn't feel any different. With each new destination, the drug-like effect of being in a new place fades faster and faster. Similar to establishing a tolerance to an external chemical influence, it appears I'll have to seek out a more potent fix. I finish my small meal and continue moving back toward the hostel.

Since this is my first communal hostel stay, everything is a learning experience. Apparently, the occupants of several rooms, male and female alike, share the bathroom at the end of the hall. The grime of a thousand travelers adheres to every crevice.

I look around after cranking the rickety, rusted faucet handle of the much-needed and anticipated shower I am about to embark upon and realize there are no towels. This isn't a hotel. I have to provide my own. I turn off the water, put my dirty clothes back on and descend the narrow staircase to the ruckus city street.

I flow in and out of a multitude of small convenience store-type shops, having little luck finding any bath items. After nearly forty minutes, I locate an overpriced tourist trap featuring fifteen-dollar ceramic replicas of the opera house and stuffed kangaroos. I purchase a gaudy yellow beach towel resembling the Australian flag.

Night falls over the fifth continent I find myself on this summer. Simultaneously, the frigid shower water falling upon my brow, absolves me of comfort.

I step with naiveté onto the Sydney streets, wandering aimlessly, equal parts tourist and vagabond. One block up, two blocks over. Each arbitrary intersection turn dictated by instantaneous whim. The clamor of a local burger joint draws me in. I find a seat and order the cheapest can of beer on the menu. A seven-dollar investment toward an evening of bad decisions.

I intentionally position myself in direct proximity to two women I find attractive. Just to my right, at the booth they occupy, sits a girl who can most efficiently be described as 'my type.' A full-sleeve tattoo covers her muscular left arm. The rest of her skin is taut and tan, undoubtedly the result of hours upon hours of outdoor physical endeavors. The form-fitting black t-shirt advertising an obscure rock band is painted on to her athletic frame. Her short dark hair frames her face perfectly. She sits across from a subtly beautiful, girl-next-door-type with an innocent smile and soft brown eyes. Her hand-made jewelry and borderline hippie attire suggests a free spirit. Her body language furthers this hypothesis. Despite a low level of commotion, I make out most of what they say.

"So what is with this guy you've been seeing?" asks the inked woman whom I'm trying hard not to stare at.

Blushing and smiling childishly, her friend responds with hesitation, "I...I...I really...I think I might be in..."

"Whoa, stop right there. You just met a few days ago. You don't even know this guy."

"I know that, but there's something so, I don't know, different."

"You two just seem so opposite. You should really slow down."

"Yeah, I mean, we are. We...I gave him the key to my place."

"You did what? Babe, that's not good. You have to be tougher than that or you're going to get crushed."

Her sweet lips want to respond. I can feel it radiating off of her, warming the drafty pub. I can hear it in her tone, how bad she wants to say, "You don't know those moments we spend, intertwined in

one another, lost in the depths of a soul we've each forever known."
Her insecurities gag her mute. She's torn. Head now low, shimmering
blonde curls cover an embarrassed girlish face.

Her friend and confidante clearly disapproves; maybe it's jealousy,
perhaps a protective response. It's tough to decipher. How easy to
maintain the third-party opinion unaffected by the sheer tenacity and
unrelenting force of that magnanimous bastard, love. That opinion
maintains a clear perspective amidst the cyclonic debris of the heart.
Bless it. Curse it. Love blinds us. It corrupts logic and heals old scar
tissue in an instant. It makes us dance naked in the rain and name
unborn grandchildren on a front porch in our twenties.

I want to interject. I want to tell her, "It doesn't matter what anyone thinks." Even if love blooms and dies in a single day, and you are
labeled a fool for the rest of your life, there's nothing in this world
more worthy of investing yourself in than love. There's nothing as
deserving the anguish it leaves in its wake. We all must die, it is the
sole certainty securely stitched into the finitely of life. What better
way to go than to let love paint the sky with your murder.

I leave cash on the table and silently make my way back into the
now-cold, caliginous twilight, to drift alone.

I flew to Sydney on a one-way ticket. Because of the lesson I
learned about onward travel at the Denver airport on my way to
Costa Rica, I'd booked my flight out of the country at the same time
to show when I'll leave.

To my surprise, I was never asked to show this at the airport. In
fact, the customs process in Australia is so streamlined that I never
saw a customs officer or had my passport stamped. I was able to
just grab my bag, scan my passport at a machine and be on my way.
The one-way departure ticket I purchased to leave Australia is for an

airport roughly 1,000 kilometers (600 miles) from Sydney, leaving in two weeks from Brisbane.

I have several transportation choices. I can rent a tiny car for around $700 plus the cost of gas, which is another $200. I can take a bus for less, or I can take a night train for $91 and spare the additional cost of a night's hostel stay.

Once again riding the rails is the most cost-effective mode of transportation. The anticipation begins to mount as I pass through the crowded Sydney railway station. The hopeful thoughts that I might be able to sit next to an attractive young lady on the trip north begin to enter my mind. It isn't long after finding my seat that a silver-haired, older woman sits beside me in. There goes that.

The ability to share common experiences, even if with a stranger, becomes more necessary the longer one travels on their own. It's easy to begin to feel disassociated from humanity when you haven't engaged in a meaningful conversation outside of your own head in weeks. It appears that little conversation will come of this leg of the trip, however.

There doesn't seem to be much commonality between the little old lady and myself.

"Is that a new tattoo?" she inquiries, pointing at the inside of my right leg.

"Yes ma'am, it's only a couple of days old."

"I like it. It's like an old fountain pen."

"Yeah, it does look like that doesn't it?" I reply, laughing a little.

"What is it supposed to be?"

"To be honest, I'm not completely sure." Laughing, I try to explain how I came to get a tattoo of something with an unknown origin. I attempt the short answer of, "I got it for charity." But this seems to confuse her.

Going further in depth, I begin to explain the adventure that Marty and I embarked upon, having to panhandle and ask for rides, sleeping outside and making it through fourteen countries in two weeks. She responds with something that catches me off guard.

"I'm homeless too."

"You don't say?" She's well kept for being homeless, but I guess I am too.

"Yeah, I sold my home and everything in it sometime back. It was hard at first but became incredibly cathartic as I reduced everything down to a few trunks."

I'm instantly fascinated. She basically tells me my own life story from her perspective. She explains how she stays with her daughter for part of the year and travels around the rest of the time.

"I'm a widow now, so I travel alone. It was a little scary at first. The first time I went to a new city by myself I thought I was going to die from the anxiety of it, but you know what? After a few days in Sydney I felt like I owned the place! Now I'm not really afraid to go places by myself. I go to the movies alone, the matinee of course, I go out to eat and enjoy the museums in different cities. Some of my friends think I'm crazy, but I don't really care. We only get one of these lives you know, and I'm not done living it just because I'm old."

Despite the age gap, we're instantly friends. For the next eight hours we talk about all the places we've been and where we want to go. We talk about how amazing the food is in Italy and how fun the old pubs are in Ireland. We talk about our favorite writers and I show her all the advantages of using an e-book.

The train rocks and sways back and forth as it rattles through the Australian countryside. The setting sun casts a kaleidoscope effect upon the sea of eucalyptus trees as our conversation flows seamlessly from topic to topic.

"Ohh, shut up you fat cunt!" A belligerent man with massive white sideburns, two rows back and across the aisle interrupts our conversation. Apparently, the woman seated behind him accidently bumped his seat as she sat back down.

"Excuse me! There's no need for that language!" she responds.

"There's no need for you to be a fat dumb cunt, either," he snaps back. Adding a very slurred warning, "Going around bumping people's seats while they're trying to sleep is a good way to get slapped in the face!"

I abruptly stop mid-sentence whatever story I'm sharing with my new friend. This guy is bold. I notice the woman's husband actually sits next to her and offers no other response than to squint his eyes a little. This is unreal. I'm not sure what's crazier, the fact that this man is screaming obscenities at a random woman on the train for no real reason, or that her husband is allowing it to happen. I'm no tough guy and I'm not married, but I'm pretty sure that man would be picking his teeth up off the floor with two broken arms if he talked that way to someone in my family.

It doesn't take long for the attendant to move the man to another seat allowing the passenger car to resume its typical mundane route. Within a few more hours the train arrives in a small town called Casino. I transfer to a bus, which takes me the rest of the way. Without as much as a goodbye, my new best friend and I step off the train and into the night. She never even told me her name.

Just before sunrise, the large charter bus rumbles into the middle of Brisbane. I still haven't looked at a map of the city. I have no clue where I'll go when I arrive. Once again, I don't have a plan or a place to stay. The first order of business, find a WiFi connection and find out where I am and what's around me. The long-sleeve shirt and shorts do little to shield me from the brisk morning air. It's winter here and I don't even own a pair of jeans, my jacket long ago surrendered to the shivering Norwegian girl in Bergen. The old saying, "Travel light, freeze at night," describes my disposition perfectly.

A quick Google search shows several inexpensive hostels within walking distance. The thought of sharing another filthy room with a half-dozen random guys in their early twenties isn't terribly appealing, but I decide to not let a single experience dictate my decisions. My nose leaks like a faucet in the frigid, uphill walk to the bright orange hostel I selected from the ones within walking distance. Brisbane City Backpackers, this is the spot. The website boasts free WiFi, a movie theater, outdoor pool, observation deck with 360 degree city views and a full bar.

It's only 7 a.m. when I arrive. Despite the check-in time being 1 p.m., I'm welcomed in and given a key to a four-person room, which cost a few dollars more than the eight or ten-person room. I figure the less people the better the smell, so I justify the additional five bucks a night.

To my surprise, I'm the only occupant of room number 18. Just me and two bunk beds for $31 a day. I haven't slept much but have a few emails to catch up on, so I put off slumber a few more hours. I order "a tall black" which apparently is Australian for "a coffee." After a few hours my eyes drift from my computer screen and observe the day has arrived. The sun eradicates the damned unpleasantness of the frosty morning temperature.

"Fuck this! I'm not sitting here all day," I proclaim aloud.

The young couple in the corner give a mild look of concern as I slam closed my old Dell laptop.

I can't remember the last time I just went for a run. It used to be one of my favorite ways to discover a new city, just get a little lost on a long run. Digging through my bag I find my last remaining pair of Ranger panties, grab my ancient RCA MP3 player and lace up my sneakers. Despite a pair of legs that feel like concrete and a lack of anything resembling an actual route, there's a lightness in my step.

The sun graciously directs itself onto my stride. It isn't long before I cross a very large bridge into an expansive world of endless possibilities.

Fortuitously, the Bob Seger song, *Roll Me Away*, travels through the short red wire into my headphones echoing the notion that I could go east or west, it's up to me to decide. I picture him staring out at the great divide on his Harley. Freedom. Absolute freedom.

Our common thread tied by classic melody. It takes five more songs for my thoughts to completely fade away. My pace slips from a run to a jog, then from a jog to a shuffle. My stomach is completely empty.

In an attempt to motivate myself to keep moving, I begin actively repeating, *I finished in the top ten overall in two different Ironman races.* My tank hits empty and I don't really know how far I've run. Just trying to keep my feet turning over is a laborious task. I notice a large gathering of people in a park. A long line of vendor tents circles the outer edge of the large grass area.

There was a time when you couldn't get me to stop in the middle of a run for anything. At first this is my mentality as I pass by the people buying food from local farmers at the market. Then I do something I've never done: I stop running. It becomes as plain to see as the day is sunny. I'm not training for anything. Possibly for the first time in my adult life. I'm not training for a combat deployment or a race or a fight or a competition. I'm just a guy out exploring a city and it's okay to stop and enjoy the day.

I spend the next half hour walking through the farmer's market conversing with strangers and enjoying the free samples offered to me. With a sweaty, five-dollar bill I placed in my sock before I leaving, I buy a small basket of strawberries and walk along the riverside for at least a mile, soaking up the sounds of the city on a cloudless Saturday morning.

Arriving back at the bright orange building where I'm staying, I lay by the pool and think of nothing for an hour. What a new experience to bask in a motionless mind. There's no weight, no pressure and no apprehension regarding the uncertainty of tomorrow or the struggle of all my yesterdays. It doesn't really matter what happens next, I don't have a plan and yet the world still spins, revolving no matter how much or how little I worry about it. Hungry or happy, mindful or mind full, reality exists entirely between these two ears.

In this life there's a single control we possess. One and only one ascendency is truly ours and that is how we choose to respond to the completely uncontrollable situations and circumstances that surround us. Live well with the knowledge that you have complete control over how you view this world and those in it. That is your greatest power—it is your only power.

The rumbling of my stomach disrupts the perfect silence of my mind. I wander inside the main building from the pool. I haven't cooked in months. The hostel's kitchen reminds me of the one at the fire station where I spent my afternoons as a child visiting my father at work. Everything is stainless steel and the fragrances of spices permeate the air, further exciting my stomach. I take a quick assessment of what's available for use in the public kitchen.

Across the street is a grocery store. I venture over and stock up on supplies. As I pace the aisles it occurs to me that it's been months since I bought groceries. What was once a streamline process becomes quite a challenge. It takes nearly an hour to fill the small, handheld basket with a few items I still feel confident enough to prepare on my own. The contents strewn out on the little black conveyer belt consist mainly of ingredients for scratch-made pancakes and a kilogram of bacon.

The simple thought of making my own bacon sandwich makes me happy. Such a simple thing, but something recently absent from my life, something I miss.

Back at the hostel, I manage to slap together a decent bacon, lettuce and tomato on toast before realizing, I didn't buy anything to wash it down.

It's Saturday evening and I'm in Australia, a country full of chaps who fancy themselves beer drinkers. Happy hour at the hostel bar features "jugs" of beer, or a pitcher where I'm from, for ten dollars.

By U.S. standards, that's actually a lot of money, but a pretty decent deal considering where I am.

The first jug goes down easy. So does the second. By the third, I'm bulletproof once again. I know if I keep up this pace I need to eat something more. The kitchen, however, is now closed. With a slight stumble, I step out to the sidewalk. Less than a hundred meters into my quest for food, I hear the overwhelming racket of a very loud, very vulgar punk band. A sign proclaiming "The Beetle Bar" hangs over the entranceway.

With a magnetic pull, I'm drawn into the establishment. A pissed-off-looking woman at the front door commands a ten-dollar cover charge. As I pull the blue bill from my wallet I ask if there will be any house music or dubstep later.

Daggers shoot from her eyes as she snatches the funny-looking money from my hand. "NO!" she snaps.

"Oh, Okay, good!" I yell over the screeching guitar in the background. Hearing my American accent and realizing my inquiry was sarcastic, she just shakes her head a little as if to say, "You're not gonna last long in there, mate."

The place reminds me of every dive bar and shitty gig I played in my late teens as a drummer. The air is stale and the floor is sticky. A dozen kids in black hoodies, who are clearly friends of the band currently playing, bounce into each other in front of the stage. A few others sit at tables along the walls, all trying desperately to look "more punk" than the people around them. Another beer quickly finds its way into my hand, and I take to my exploration of the small venue.

"Fuck you fucking cunt, fuck you fucking cunt, fuck you fucking cunt!" screams the tiny female vocalist on stage as the bass player flails around dramatically, wearing nothing but a thong and a couple of ironically placed pieces of black electrical tape over his nipples. A few songs later their set concludes. I walk around in shorts and flip-flops, as out of place as a Bible salesmen in Iran. The looks I receive don't bother me. I've spent so much time in places like this.

After a few more beers and a couple more bands featuring more energy and showmanship than talent, I remember the reason I left the first bar. I was hungry. Now I'm drunk and hungry. Lacking the simple logic that comes with sobriety, I return to the hostel where I'm staying. As I make my way to the locked kitchen to attempt a break in, a girl in her early twenties stops me. Her lip piercing complements her jet-black hair and tattoos perfectly. She has a clipboard in her hands with a short list of names on it. She's the same one behind the counter when I checked in. I'm busted.

"You were lying by the pool earlier weren't you?" she asks.

"Yeah, that was me."

"How would you like to participate in an all-male review?"

"What? Like strip?"

"Yeah! We're doing it here at the bar in a little bit. The winner gets $100."

"I'm not sure my grandmother would approve of me stripping for money."

"Well, you only get the money if you win."

"That isn't better."

"I don't think you will have a problem, I saw you earlier with your shirt off. Take a look around. You've got this."

"Thank you for the vote of confidence, but I'm a bit shy and taking my clothes off in front of a bar full of people may not go over well."

"Too bad. Your name is on the list."

"Well, it appears I don't have much of a choice in the matter then, eh?"

Once again, my quest for food is detoured. The first contestant takes the stage and clearly has a blood alcohol level higher than his IQ. After him comes another drunk guy who's never seen the inside of a gym, followed by another and another. I'm not saying I'm proud of it, but I take advantage of a short break before my turn to go knock out a few pushups. I want to get that quick pump, cause you know, I'm a tool.

Each guy picks a girl to put in the hot seat on stage and strips for them. When my name is finally called, I walk directly to the girl with the clipboard and inform her, "You got me into this mess, you're gonna get me out of it! Sit your ass down right there!"

I decide I'm way too drunk to make a handstand walk entrance. These situations are about confidence, so I put on my best 'general-on-a-battlefield' persona and place my right shoe on her left thigh.

"Take it off!" I command over the music.

She hesitantly obliges and removes both of my shoes. Standing over her lap, I demand she unbutton my pants and unzip me. At this point, any embarrassment I may have felt shifts to her.

Laughing awkwardly she concedes to the order. The pants come off, next is the shirt, and I commence to ride her like a rodeo cowboy. It doesn't last much longer, but the crowd eats the whole show up. Apparently, I'm the last participant and after a short deliberation from all of the ladies in the establishment it's determined: I'm the rightful winner of the grand prize.

With everyone cheering I gather my pants, couldn't find my dignity, and am handed $100 Australian dollars. Immediately I hold up the money and proclaim that every girl in the bar gets a drink on me. This entire time traveling alone has been difficult for me to make new friends, when apparently all I had to do was strip down to my underwear, grind around for a bit, then buy everyone a drink. As the ladies enjoy their free libation, I step out of the hostel bar to find something to eat, one last time. ✸

CHAPTER SEVENTEEN

Old Habits

"I was not designed to be forced. I will breathe after my own fashion. Let us see who is the strongest."—Henry David Thoreau

Fully clothed, I awake atop the thin green blanket, head pounding. Begrudgingly, my eyes peel open and I scan the small stale room. My hands keep warm tucked deeply in the pockets of my shorts. As I remove my right hand it grazes a small piece of paper.

Clumsily, I pull the slip up to my face, eyes still adjusting to the light.

Is that a comma?…$1,094…What the fuck did I buy for…Holy shit… that's my bar tab from the last place I went last night! My bar tab has a comma in it!

After a month of not letting that animal out of its cage, it apparently had some pent-up energy to burn. The pieces of the rest of the night start to come back as I begin sifting through my backpack for my toothbrush. There were the three Australian ladies who derailed me from my mission to find something to eat. There was a guy from Buffalo, New York, who joined our group after seeing the three-to-one ratio. *Did I really buy that much champagne?* The band was really good at least. At least I think they were pretty good.

When I notice what time it is, I realize I slept in past checkout. If I was staying in a nice hotel this wouldn't be an issue, but this is a backpacker hostel, which means I'll be paying for another night. I know I don't want to spend the next week and a half here in the city, especially with the sting of such an intensely frivolous evening echoing through my splitting head.

A quick search shows a pickup location about ten kilometers away where I can rent a small campervan. I begin to imagine the limitless freedom and lasting adventures I can create. After a pot of coffee and some pancakes, I stumble into the blinding light of the afternoon sun, still in the same clothes I slept in and embark on an hour-long urban hike.

I'm almost sober by the time I arrive at the rental place. The parking lot is full of the most hideous green and purple vans with, "Don't you wish yo campa was hot like me?" painted on the side panel in obnoxious bubble letters. It actually costs less to rent a van with a full bed, DVD player and a mini-kitchen than a tiny, two-door car, now I know why. It looks like someone ate their weight in Skittles and puked all over the outside of these hideous vehicles.

By the time I leave the rental office the $25-a-day van doubles in price due to the required insurance not mentioned on the website. I despise this type of deception, but it's the way of the world. To get mad about it does no good. I do what I do and make a joke out of my discourse, "That means I can go off road with this bitch then yeah?" My sarcasm is lost on the young man handing me the keys to the emesis basin on wheels.

"Maybe you should read that rental agreement again," he informs me, flatly. He takes the time to show me every mundane feature of the ugly little wagon. My drunken state quickly shifts to an extreme hangover making everything he says drag on. I'd pay a million dollars for a Gatorade and a nap right now and this guy won't shut up about how to use the tiny little stove in the back. After what feels like the entire last day of school when you were twelve years old, he hands me the keys.

"Ya got any questions, mate?"

"Umm, yeah, it looks like some joker put the steering wheel on the wrong side in this one. Can we get that fixed real quick?"

"Yeah, I'll let 'em know, mate."

A quick trip back to the hostel to collect my belongings and I'm on my way. While in Thailand, several Australians told me that Byron Bay is the spot to go on Australia's east coast. It's roughly two hundred kilometers south of where I stayed in Brisbane. The open road and a full tank of gas is one of the most easily accessible and often neglected forms of freedom.

Two hours of driving and my senses come alive with the salty smell of the sea. Byron is a lively little backpacker haven. Trendy shops and restaurants line the streets. Something seems familiar about the strangers strolling down the sidewalk. The majority has a slow easy step moving toward nothing at all. No hustle, no rush, just a bunch of other dry leaves letting the wind carry them around the world.

The idea of sleeping in this ugly little van excites me. Every ideal-looking spot to post up for the evening, however, has a sign threatening high fines for sleeping in your vehicle. Seems reasonable in a park, but finding a spot anywhere becomes increasingly difficult. After a short conversation with a random stranger I learn it's illegal to car camp everywhere in this area.

It's getting dark and the sleep I had the night before wasn't exactly the restful sort. The weight of my eyelids triples in just a few moments. After another hour of driving circles just outside of town, a sign jumps out at me like a kangaroo. "Camping." Simple, yet effective, advertising. Pulling into what's little more than a large grass lot the size of about two football fields, I notice a dozen other small motorhomes and vans parked sporadically. This looks like home for the night. While converting the two bench seats in the back into a bed, and heating up some soup, a guy in his early twenties approaches me about the ten-dollar nightly fee. I pay happily, make short work of the large bowl of stew and open the moonroof allowing the radiant beauty of a million shining stars to illuminate and fill the back of the small van.

The next morning, as the single gas stove boils the water for my coffee, I walk over to the camp's only facility to fill a jug of water to wash my dishes. A kind-looking, older gentleman sits on a weathered camp chair just outside his seasoned RV. He could be retired, seems about the right age and doesn't maintain the constant state of concern which those gainfully employed individuals tend to. He introduces himself as Malcolm and tells me he's come to this spot for several years. An odd place to make an intentional returning pilgrimage. My stay is out of necessity and lack of bearings on free places to camp. I'm brief, yet polite, in conversation, not wanting my coffee to boil over.

After a modest breakfast of eggs and toast, I decide the day's mission will be to find a surfboard and once again try my hand at riding a wave.

Popping red and blue lights ignite my rear view mirror at just past ten o'clock this morning, as I drive five kilometers under the speed limit through a quiet residential neighborhood. At first I think the van I rented has a brake light out or something else of a simple nature. Despite the thought that this is a routine traffic stop, the pulse of my heart jumps.

Without removing his full-face helmet, the motorcycle officer approaches my vehicle and requests my driver's license. I comply respectfully, addressing him as "Sir" and producing everything he asks for.

"You went past me with your seatbelt off back there," he mumbles through the facemask on his helmet.

"Yes, sir. I usually don't wear it."

"Where are you from?"

"I'm from the U.S., sir."

"How long have you been here?"

"Not long at all, sir. I rented this van yesterday."

"It's against the law to not wear a seat belt here."

"Really? Hmm. I apologize, sir. I honestly did not realize that. I haven't seen any signs."

"Well, you're getting a ticket regardless. It's against the law. This will only be a second, I'll be right back."

I can't believe it. A ticket seems a little harsh for a foreign traveler for the sole offense of not wearing a seat belt. The quick second he's to be gone, turns into a couple of minutes. I notice the officer arguing with a cyclist passing by. I can't help but laugh as, without removing his helmet, the officer verbally thrashes another grown man for riding his bike on the sidewalk. He brandishes the ticket book and is about to issue another absurd citation. The offending party apologizes profusely and explains that he's having a bad day and is allowed to continue on as long as he walks his bike. He was just told that he's not allowed to ride without a helmet.

At this point, I begin to look for a hidden camera. This has to be a joke. Through the van's side mirror I see him writing out my ticket. Not more than thirty seconds later a woman passes by on an old cruiser bicycle. For the second time, the uniformed man stops in the middle of writing my fine to harass a citizen for riding on the sidewalk. After an exchange, the woman changes paths and is made to ride with the traffic in the now-busy road. You have to be kidding me! This guy still hasn't shown his face to the last three people he's stopped. So far not one has actually created anything close to a hazard for anyone else.

The third and final cyclist he stops is a little old woman riding in the street without a helmet on. The masked man harasses her for a few minutes before making her pull a helmet from her bag and put it on before being allowed to continue the remainder of her 400-meter trip to the market. When the civil servant returns to the driver's side window of my rented car, he bestows upon me a ticket, a ticket for $311 dollars.

"That...that is a lot of money, sir!"

"Yeah, but not wearing your seatbelt is a serious offense."

"Really? How's that?"

"We have four main causes of personal injury in this area; drinking and driving, fatigued drivers, speeding, and people not wearing seat belts."

"I understand the first three because of potential danger to others, but I'm not asking anyone else to assume any possible harm if I don't wear a seat belt."

"You could get hurt if you don't."

"That's my choice though. Just like it's the choice of those people who weren't wearing helmets. All of us are adults and assume the responsibility of our own actions as a result. Any amount is egregious to fine a private citizen for making a choice that impacts only their personal well-being exclusively, but over three hundred dollars is beyond egregious, it is asinine, sir."

"Well, in the last twenty-four years I've seen seat belts save lives. They keep you safe."

"That isn't the point here, sir. The point is that my safety is my personal choice. I'd love to see the statistics of how many people a year have adverse medical issues associated with smoking or eating fast food compared to vehicular harm, yet they're not ticketed for those choices. People aren't ticketed for having unprotected sex or drinking excessive amounts of alcohol at home. None of those things are safe. There's no logic in charging a person for committing an act that is in no way hazardous to anyone but the person committing the act other than an informal taxation."

"Here's your ticket. There's a website on the back if you want to complain."

The man without a face returns to his patrol bike and speeds off to catch another "criminal."

Why do laws exist? To ensure the protection of our citizens. Should that protection include protecting individuals from themselves? No. If an adult of legal age chooses with a clear mind and sound knowledge of potential repercussion to engage in an activity that will in no way create harm to others, but has a potential to create harm upon themselves, that's their right. Eating copious amounts of refined sugar is directly linked with diabetes, a disease that kills more than five times more people a year than accidents involving unrestrained drivers. Not only does the government not fine you outrageous amounts for consuming the toxic substances, they actually subsidize them, making them easier to access.

If a person drives drunk they present a known hazard to others, which is why we created a law forbidding the action. It is not legal to discharge a firearm into the air because of the potential to hurt or kill another person. I can't legally walk up and strike another human being without legal reprisal, because my freedom to do what I want ends at the starting point of the freedoms of those who surround me. I can, however, smoke a cigarette, despite the fact that it will kill me. As long as I don't do it around other people, inevitably putting those at risk without consent.

The creation of and enforcement of such a law delegitimizes the nature of law enforcement. Do we need laws? Yes. Do we need those laws to be enforced? Absolutely. Do we need agencies creating restrictions on our personal freedoms for the sole purpose of generating income for the state? No, but that's the only reason I was pulled over today. A government mismanages its resources then extorts more from its citizens, or in this case its tourists, in the name of protecting them.

That is what traveling is all about though, I suppose; identifying the various nuances and idiosyncrasies of other nations and cultures. It can be dreadfully annoying at times, a bit overwhelming and apparently quite costly. All being legitimate reasons to stay home where you know the rules and where you know it's safe, although this exact same thing happens in the United States on a regular basis. Personally, I'm going to take the $311 ticket, frame it next to the letter banning me from Notre Dame University for life and the speeding ticket I got on my bicycle for going 48 in a 25, if I ever have a wall again, and chalk it up as another expensive life lesson.

The trendy boutiques and chic restaurants pass by me on both sides. Taunt tan bodies carry glassed chunks of foam, with a contradictorily energetic, yet lackadaisical step, toward the billowing echoes of the salty howling sea, repeatedly infusing itself into endless stretches of glistening white sand. Byron Bay has a pulse all its own; a reminiscent hangover of a foregone hippy paradise scantily exposed and yet fully exploited in capitalistic intent.

A forced ease radiates from the predominantly transient populace. It's often difficult in towns like this to discern between the genuinely free spirits and the ones trying their damndest to appear that way. The popular backpacker's destination already buzzes this morning, as shops gouge patrons, and attractive women in their early twenties attempt to sell expensive tour packages to out-of-towners. Yoga girls mingle with surfer guys between the various juice bars and kebab huts.

The town has no shortage of surf shops, yet none of them feels right to me. I continue driving just outside of town and spot a hand-painted sign advertising surfboards. Pulling in, I notice a dozen or so boards haphazardly strewn about the front lawn of the somewhat dilapidated, hut-like establishment. A genuine authenticity subtly speaks to me as I step out of the little green van. In a thick Australian accent, a fit man in his mid-fifties greets me. His face seems weathered in the distinguished way telling of a life fully lived, and more often than not, appreciated greatly. The lines of his face are the smiling type. It's not quite noon as he stands up from what used to be a van bench seat now placed like lawn furniture. I see the large beer in his hand. He slurs with the confidence of a man who's no stranger to A.M. libating.

"Ey, mate. I'm Mic Dawg. You looking for a board?"

"Yes, sir. I am."

The conversation that follows lasts for well over two hours and has nothing to do with surfboards. I listen intently as Mic unravels a series of unique and flowing verse. He claims to have composed fifty thousand poems, many of which he committed to memory. Mic, a Zen Buddhist, shares my affinity for not only poetry, but perspective as well.

"Money, what is that, mate. It's not real, ya know. It's feathers on a peacock, mate. It's all for show. It's all just to impress the birds, ya know. All show, all flash. What matters is in here and how we treat each other."

It isn't preachy, his delivery. He means it, all of it, down to his core. Mic tells me about his own nomadic background and how nine years prior he purged all of his earthly possessions, down to the clothes on his back and went to the Outback to teach English and poetry to Aboriginals. I thought the meager contents of my single backpack made me a minimalist. Mic's story further inflates my perspective.

He offers to take me surfing, having not even attempted to sell me a board. I come to find out that he doesn't own the place, or even work there. It's his friend's shop. Without hesitation, I purchase a dinged up, used board and conclude the best way to scrub your self of one negative interaction is to be open to a positive one. I'd pulled up to the rustic roadside shop with a rather rancid, rancor-type taste in my mouth for most things human and left with an invigorated zeal. A single conversation, a single interaction with another human, has an astounding ability to redirect our outward display toward others. A chain-reaction effect herein, spreading contagiously throughout our myriad experience and rippling like a still pond stone throw.

My attempts to use the board, unfortunately, are not as productive as my experience purchasing it. The frigid water washes over my frozen feet and feeble attempts to simply stand up. I've done this before with relative success, yet for some reason, today feels like the first time.

Surfing is, single-handedly, the most rewarding, frustrating, silly, spiritual, ever-evolving endeavor my mind has set to master. An hour of failing here is better than a day of success almost anywhere else. An hour is all my numb limbs can withstand. It's summer where I'm from, but down under winter has had its way with the otherwise warm waves.

I pack it in and head back to the campground. On my way back, I make a supply stop at Woolworth grocery store and purchase a can of chunky soup and instant rice. On my way out of the store a giant green box catches my attention. Hoyts Kiosk, a Redbox-esk movie dispensary.

I can't remember the last time I just sat and watched a movie. I stand in the short line between two patchouli-clad knock off beatniks and a stoned skater. I rent a couple of movies and retreat to the quiet sanctity of the large grass lot behind the rugby field.

As the sun sets on a day more interesting than productive, I open the back hatch of the rented van and fire up the small single-burner stove, stowed conveniently under the rest of the compact conversion kitchen. The meager meal is made in minutes. I pop in one of the movies to the TV/DVD combo featured in the van's ceiling compartment and settle in for an uneventful evening.

Just as Matthew McConaughey's character has his first volatile interaction with a gay man in *Dallas Buyer's Club*, I hear a faint tap on the van door.

My first thought is this must be the camp attendant coming around to collect the ten-dollar fee as he did at approximately the same time last night. To my surprise it's an older gentleman. At second glance, I notice it's Malcolm, the man I spoke with briefly before leaving the park this morning.

"Hey mate, wacha into?"

Thinking this a bit odd, I respond, "Just watching a movie."

"Ohh yeah, a good one is it?"

What is he doing here? Does he need something? I think to myself.

At this very moment I notice Malcolm's fly is down and his dick is hanging halfway out. I make every effort to maintain strict eye contact, not wanting him to see that I just caught a glance of his shriveled pee shooter. In the event his exposed trouser snake is an accident, I calmly ask, "How's your night going."

"Good yeah...So good movie then yeah?"

"Yup."

"Ahh good, good mate," he repeats in an awkward, but rehearsed way. "So you feeling horny then?" he asks, while performing a not-so-subtle pelvic tilt to ensure once and for all that I'm well aware his dick slip is no fluke.

Bold move, Malcolm... Bold move, indeed.

"No, I'm good," I start pulling the sliding door closed shut, nearly snagging his wang in the process, "Just gonna finish watching this movie. Have yourself a good evenin...." The door lock engages before I finish my sentence.

Not sure if you've ever been propositioned for sex by a geriatric man in a foreign country, but it has a bit of a paralytic effect. I know

I have a lot of friends who say they'd punch the man in the face, but in all honesty, an event like this is such a surprise, such a shock to the system, it's difficult to digest.

The reality of what just occurred begins to sink in and I make sure every door is locked. The way that necessary bodily functions do, mine alerts me of a need to micturate at what is now the least opportune time to step outside.

My thoughts are consumed with my bloated bladder. *My back teeth are floating! I'm not going out there now though. That man was* FORWARD! I peek out of the tiny curtains with mental images of Malcolm hiding behind a bush with a bottle of chloroform waiting to pounce on me.

Is this why he's been coming here for years? Is this some kind of gay orgy park? Ohh man, my fucking luck, I pick the gay orgy camp ground while down the road there's probably some hippie yoga chick massage party going on.

I can't hold it in any more. I have to pee. It's been twenty-minutes, it's probably safe now. A gallon of toxic fluid sloshes around about to burst in my abdomen. Quick check left and right. Still getting a bit of a rapey vibe, but I don't see any creeps. *Ohh man, what if there are more Malcolms out there?*

Like a special operations interdiction mission, I slide the door open with speed and silence, making haste for the front bumper. I'm not about to walk past Malcolm's mobile residence to the toilets, no way.

In a panicked fury I spray the tire and front end of the vehicle like a feral cat. Scanning left and right intently, I push with the violent force known to cause hernias. A liter and a half of fluid has never in history exited a pin-sized hole so fast.

The next morning I peer through the beam of light between the grey curtain and window seam. He's gone. That creep packed up and left in the night. Off to create more lasting emotional scars in the minds of unsuspecting victims, no doubt. It was going to make for an awkward, pre-coffee conversation if that pervert had still been hanging out.

I'm not going to hang around to find out if he comes back. The camp attendant never came around to collect the ten dollars. Typically, I'd spend the time to track him down and pay the fee, but not this time. I can't be gone fast enough. Furthermore, I feel like I endured ten-dollars worth of mental anguish to justify skipping out on the bill.

For the time, I'm done with the underground Australian sex camps. I decide to fork over the twenty dollars for another hostel room close to the town center. Conveniently located and crawling distance from several adult drinking establishments, Holiday Village Backpackers suffices as well as any of the other frat-like establishments in town.

I pay the extra few dollars for the four-person room, and once again have it to myself. I park the van and take to further exploring the town. By just past sun down, I hear the sounds of live music coming from what looks like an old train depot. A female performer with a sultry voice entertains a growing crowd of beer enthusiasts in the front patio area. Patrons warm their hands over trash can fires, which add to the hobo-chic ambiance of the Railway Bar.

I secure a pint of local beer and take my position as a lonely observer, overhearer of conversations I wish to be a part of, a generally awkward guy by himself at the bar on a Saturday night. A voluptuous brunette makes her rounds, flirting with every guy willing to engage her in conversation. She stays engaged to each just long enough for them to take interest, buy her a drink and then moves on to the next. Some type of needy I have no stomach for.

"Are you Canadian?" she slurs, barely keeping her fruity drink in its container. A sad effort at making me her next target.

"Are you a Kiwi?" Knowing she's Australian, this will piss her off.

Hearing my accent she retorts, "Ohh, you're American, yeah that figures."

I correct her, "Technically, Canadians are Americans, too." It's evident she doesn't understand the concept that America is a continent, two actually.

"You know what's wrong with America?"

I pause in anticipation of what I'm sure is about to be a sophomoric drunk diatribe about guns and imperialism. As she starts in slurring and bashing over-three-hundred million people, I interrupt her and inquire, "Have you ever actually been to the United States?" Of course, her response is, that she has not. Engaging this overgrown, sorority queen in intellectual debate on the topic of international relations and the various geopolitical spheres which led to our current state is something analogous to starting a bare-knuckle fist fight with a third grader.

Before I make up my mind, a random man interjects himself into the conversation from over my left shoulder, "Fuck this cunt." I shift attention to the overtly blunt, bearded man. "Some of the best people I know are from the U.S. I lived there for twelve years, mate. They're a lot of fake cunts around here and this bitch is one of them. Never been anywhere, but have opinions about everywhere."

He introduces himself as Damien. He sways like he's standing on a boat in a storm. As I reflect on the weight of what was said and begin to respond to Damien, he leans forward and grabs the breasts of the older woman standing to his left. An action which shifts the energy surrounding the makeshift fire pit. To my surprise, he manages the act without facing the consequences of physical violence. Disbelief mixed with mild arousal overcomes the contours of the woman's face and as quickly as it began, my conversation with Damien ends, as he now exchanges pleasantries with the person I was sure would have slapped him.

Once again, I'm left to the ignorant ramblings of the plastic woman to my right. She tells me everything she dislikes about George Bush.

I remind her, "He hasn't been president for a long time."

She tells me about how guns are stupid and pointless and no one should have them.

I ask, "Have you ever fired a weapon?" I'm not surprised when she says no. The less interested and more annoyed I become with this troll, the more she wants to talk to me. I have to break away. There's absolutely no point in attempting a reasonable and logic-based conversation with an obnoxious, opinionated drunk. It's a buzzkill, and in a place where a beer costs eight dollars, my buzz is valuable.

I manage to break free from her uneducated tirade under the guise of needing to piss, and slip off into the night. Leaving the bar, I choose to continue walking away from the hostel I'm staying in.

A couple of blocks later I hear the distinct sound of a fight about to commence. A type of vitriol with its own particular wavelength. I'm sure I am going to have to defend a young French girl outside of a pizza place as she's verbally accosted by three intoxicated young men. As soon as I play the chivalry card and interject myself between the drunken pack and her, I realize, she's the instigator of the conflict. She screams at the three Australian twenty year olds, demanding they give her a cigarette.

One of the boys pulls his dick from his pants, shaking it violently in the middle of the street and yells, "I don't have a cigarette, but I got a dick! You want this little thing? It's all you Frenchie!"

A boy clearly enamored by her vile, entitled demeanor steps in to defend her. She furthers my belief that not all women are worth protecting when she spits on her white knight and stumbles down an alleyway.

All the while, the pimple-faced pizza shop worker looks on, unimpressed.

"Typical night for you, eh?" I inquire, positioning myself for a late night treat.

"Man, I've seen things."

The humanity of the night continues to dissipate outside of a bar called Cheeky Monkeys, as I bear witness to more of what I can only describe as a battle for the title of 'bottom of the human race' unfolds in a vibrant showing, displaying the impact of reality television on society.

Stepping inside I conclude that Byron Bay is little more than a little rich girls tourist trap, cleverly disguised as a funky hippy beach community. My conversation with the bartender keeps me from judging the whole of the area, based on what I observe here.

"Get off the beaten path," he says, "talk to people, learn something."

He gives the advice at the heels of my statement, "This is the single-most, douche-infected place I have been throughout my travels." Early the next morning, I heed his advice and leave the sorority party called Byrons Bay. ✹

CHAPTER EIGHTEEN

Paradise Lost, or at Least Left

*"My manners, abominable at times, can be sweet. As I grew older I became
a drunk. Why? Because I like the ecstasy of the mind. I'm a wretch.
But I love, love."*—Jack Kerouac

I drive for hours looking for a place to park 'Skittle vomit' for the
evening, when I notice a small group of people playing basketball
from the road. The hand-painted sign out front reads: Backpacker's
Paradise. A confident claim to make, if you ask me. My original plan
is to just sleep in the van. However, this place looks like a lot of fun.
I make a snap decision, an illegal U-turn, and squeeze into the tiny
subterranean parking lot.

A half-dozen green picnic tables line the outside of the multipur-
pose courtyard, divided by a volleyball net. The sign on the office
door states: Closed, visit the bar for assistance. Across the courtyard
is a small open-air bar with a half-dozen stools and a few old couches.
A billiards and foosball table entertain a small group of travelers just
in front of the small pub. This place seems perfect.

"Who do I pay?" I ask the young woman propped up against the
register behind the bar.

"What would you like?"

"How about a beer and a room?"

"We can do both."

Apparently it's happy hour, meaning the beer is $3.50 a can. The room adds twenty-nine more Australian dollars to the tab. Both costs are significantly less than most of the other places I've recently seen in the area. After being shown to my room I take advantage of a quick shower. After a few days of surfing and sleeping in the back of a van, the ten minutes spent under the stream of hot water makes me feel like a human again.

Exhausted and excited about the notion of an actual bed, I'm asleep within a half hour of arriving. Twelve hours later I wake to the crisp, gentle ocean breeze pushing through the open window above me, tickling my nose. I hear a few other residents playing in the courtyard below. Invigorated, my step pops as I glide down the stairs to a cup of coffee in the public kitchen. The communal cooking no longer feels foreign. The bustle of early morning hostel living already feels natural and comforting.

With a fresh long black, I take to my laptop. It's been a while since sitting to purposefully write. My recent lack of creative activity has me feeling restless. The previous months were transformative, an awkward evolution from athlete to author. It hasn't been until just recently that I feel natural telling people, "I'm a writer," when met with inquiries about my profession. For the first time I actually see myself this way and not as the athlete I previously was.

After a couple of hours at the keyboard, a guy named Luke staggers into the little hostel bar where I'm writing and shoots me an evil grin.

In the thickest English accent I've heard in a while, Luke asks, "What are you doing?"

"Just writing a little."

"Ahh cool. You should come wit me to Hooters then, yeah!"

"Pardon?"

"Yeah mate, I was just thea, fixing to go back. Let's get pissed, yeah!"

"I was going to catch a surf."

"Yeah, yeah, you could do tha butcha not. You gonna come wit me to Hooters and get pissed."

"Okay then. I suppose that's settled then. Let me put up my laptop and we'll go."

"Ahh, fuck yeah, then!"

Luke is from Liverpool, but has been living in New Zealand for some time. He recently relocated to Australia to find work and is taking advantage of the transitional downtime. Luke is in pretty good shape with a build that suggests he grew up playing sports. He has a full sleeve tattoo and holds no reservation about approaching a perfect stranger to tell them, not ask them, to grab a drink. He has the right balance of charm and in-your-face, no-nonsense that I like in a drinking buddy.

I haven't had a wingman for a very long time, so despite having a pretty substantial dislike for Hooters, I'm eager to see where this will go. Luke isn't the shy type, combined with a propensity for day drinking, this could go just about anywhere.

I find out quickly that my initial impression of the Englishmen is spot on. We haven't even made it the fifteen steps from the front door to our respective seats and he's already hit on three of the girls working. The terrible, overpriced food and shitty service go unnoticed for me during this visit.

For six straight hours we go back and forth on shots and beers, swapping stories and flirting with the well-endowed woman behind the bar. The more we drink, the heavier Luke's accent gets. I start translating his drink order for the Aussie bird behind the bar. He orders a double brandy, rocks and she looks at me with that, "What the hell did he just say?" look plastered all over her face. So the English-speaking American becomes the translator between the English-speaking guy from the U.K. and the English-speaking woman from Australia.

Six hours, and a few hundred dollars, goes by a lot faster at a bar than I could ever make it go at work. After Luke proposes marriage to the third girl in under an hour, I decide that it may be best to close out our tabs and walk the few blocks back to the hostel for happy hour. With an amalgamation of swagger and stumble, we enter the hostel's courtyard.

"Were you guys at Hooters that entire time?" one of the young ladies asks with judgment beaming from her wide eyes.

"Gotta have lunch somewhere." I reply, sarcastically.

I post up, beer in one hand, Kindle in the other. Less than a page into Thoreau's *Civil Disobedience* my reading is interrupted.

"What are you reading?"

"Nothing that you want to get me rambling about," I respond, peeling my eyes from the glowing screen just long enough to see the inquisitor is an attractive short, blond girl in her mid-twenties.

I noticed her immediately when I walked into the open court of the hostel for the first time last night. I can tell she's from Canada from the subtle way she alters the delivery of the word "about." She's, far and away, the cutest girl I've seen in awhile. Each time I saw her in the courtyard in the last twenty-four hours she received plenty of attention from the male guests. A colorful feather braided into her golden hair, that I'd find silly on most people, somehow works perfectly for her. It's clear she's an athlete. Toned curves hugged by perfectly-tanned skin. For some reason, for all of her attractive physical attributes it's her calves I noticed first. I know this seems odd, and I can't explain it exactly, but that's what caught my attention at first glance. I learn through a short conversation they are the product of sprinting up and down a basketball court for years, confirming my beliefs about her athletic background.

The plans Luke and I made to go out on an organized bar crawl dissipate quickly. I find myself genuinely captivated by this person, now sitting across from me on this green bench, under the blooming Australian stars. The hours pass in the matter of a few breaths. She buys me a beer and we share stories until the small bar closes at ten o'clock.

"Let's find a real bar," I suggest.

"Let's!" she replies, without hesitation.

A quirky, yet uninvited third-party, finds his way into our conversation. An otherwise interesting man with a slim build, slight German accent and thin, red beard. He invites himself on our quest to find a pub, a fact I am not overly zealous about, but welcome the additional conversation and opportunity to learn more about his background. Our newly founded trio leisurely strolls through the streets of the small coastal town appropriately named Surfers Paradise.

Sitting in a posh little bar we learn our new German friend is actually from Chile and fluent in three languages. I also learn that our 5' 2" Canadian companion lived in Panama earlier this year. My idea to switch the conversation to Spanish in an effort to impress her is terribly nearsighted. I've spoken nothing but English for months now, and even when I spoke Spanish every day I wasn't very good at it. Add the fact that my body is doing its very best to process the fifteen or so drinks polluting my blood and my foreign conversational skill can hardly be discerned.

It isn't long before the bar closes and we once again search for someplace to add gas to the fire. The sound of Dr. Dre leaping from the inside of another establishment is magnetic, attracting my attention. Before I know it we're on the dance floor, enabling me to flaunt my awkward, lack of coordination and general seizure-like movements that resemble dancing. If she isn't impressed by my overall homeless-looking appearance, mastery of the Spanish language, equivalent to a three-year-old Mexican kid with a learning disability, and propensity for vulgarity, then these dance moves are sure to draw her in.

Only three drinks later, our third bar of the evening closes. Not being the kind of person to forego junk food after nearly two-dozen drinks, we stop off for a late night snack. I manage to get almost half of the contents of the kebab into my stomach. The Hansel-and-Gretel-style trail of meat and lettuce mark the path back to the hostel. Our Chilean friend quickly makes his way back to his room leaving the two of us in the courtyard. There's only one logical thing to do now. Only one thing makes sense to a guy who's been drinking all day and is now alone with a woman whom he finds both interesting and beautiful.

"I'm jumping in the pool! You're coming with me."

"What? It's freezing!"

She must be slightly less drunk than I am, because to me it seems completely logical. The four-foot fence is no match for my fitness level. In all honestly, it's a miracle that I don't fall face first on the concrete as I leap the small, black metal obstacle. Sobriety smacks me in the face, the instant my naked skin is wrapped in that freezing liquid blanket. I manage to avoid the girlish audible screech typically associated with such a sudden drop in comfort.

"Didn't you say you were going to give me a towel?"

"I never said that, no."

"Hmmm, okay. It's a little cold though, so maybe you could help me out a little." I'm trying hard not to shiver, as if being cold makes me look weak. I hop back over the fence and sit next to her on the steps that lead up to my room.

The nature of the situation wakes me up. It's four o'clock in the morning, I've been getting along great with this girl for over seven hours and now the two of us sit completely alone in the dark. To be honest, I hate this moment. There's no other moment that carries this level of self-doubt.

Does she actually like me? Did she laugh at my jokes because she's being polite or flirty? What's going through her mind right now? Does she think me cowardly for not taking the reins, for not slipping my hand behind her head and pulling her closely into me? Or is she waiting for the opportunity to excuse herself, and go to bed?

In the seventeen or so years since the first time I found myself in a moment like this, it hasn't ever become easier. It has never become less tense. In all the world, this moment is universally difficult. A lifetime can pass within each uncomfortable tick of the clock.

Few things in this world are as simple and satisfying as the smell of a beautiful woman's hair on your pillow. The world stops momentarily as I indulge in the pleasure of each soft inhalation. I know that very shortly the door will open and there will be no mention of what just happened. We will return to the group of travelers and act like nothing happened, but this moment is mine. Naked human skin has its own unique heat pattern. I revel in its warmth for as long as I can. One last long kiss before the search begins for the random articles of clothing, which exploded like a grenade a few hours ago.

In a similar manner, just as the morning before, we individually make our way into the kitchen and begin making coffee. The scent of bacon melts into the sound of exaggerated stories from everyone's Saturday night. Laughing and joking like old friends, the stainless steel room begins to feel less like a random kitchen in a foreign country and more like the fire station I grew up in back in Peoria, Arizona.

When it comes time to depart, I hand over the surfboard I bought in Byron Bay to a young traveler who expressed an interest in learning and unceremoniously give myself to the road once again.

By the time I arrive back in Brisbane my immune system fully surrenders to the compounding germs of countless close quarters throughout the multi-continent road trip. Viscous, green sludge backstops my airway and a small group of miners aggressively dig for precious metals inside my head. I return the van and search for a hotel for the evening. My condition demands private quarters and a hot shower. It's possible to possess the capacity to snap a bone, rip the flesh from sinew, or sustain a cataclysmic shock to the skull without so much as a flinch, yet somehow, an invisible microscopic bug drags the toughest of men to their knees and initiates a whimpering for the comfort of their mother.

By morning the cranial hammering amplifies to the chaotic symphony of a construction site. The nasal sludge now solidifies to a concrete consistency. International travel in today's hyper-paranoid climate is already mind numbingly frustrating, trudging through the process with a high-grade fever is enough to make even the most magnanimous of men wish the harshest ill will toward all of humanity.

Cramming myself into the ever-shrinking, economy class seat, I attempt to settle in for an uncomfortable evening among the stars, above a foreign ocean, en route to Christchurch, New Zealand. ❀

CHAPTER NINETEEN

Kiwis and Coffee

"Every man is guilty of all the good he did not do."—Voltaire

Central America, Europe, Thailand, and Australia are all in my rearview mirror. In each I left a piece of myself, of my preconceived notions about a place and the people in it. Each place became a part of me, and my continued outlook on how I'll view the next series of circumstances throughout the course of life's journey.

Stepping off the plane in the middle of the night in Christchurch, New Zealand, my head throbs as the infection in my sinuses grows stronger and my fever steadily climbs higher. I receive a new message from a friend back home. He's in a state of distress and considering taking drastic actions. Sometime between the last time I accessed the Internet and now, an article I wrote on suicide was published, causing a strong and vocal public reaction. In the article, I took the hardest line against taking your own life as I could muster, referring to suicide as a cowardly act, and in turn those who commit the act, cowards. The intent behind the hard words was to reach a very specific audience, an audience which often times only responds to hard words, an audience that holds the notion of being a coward at the highest levels of contempt; the military veteran community.

At this time, an epidemic of veteran suicide plagues my peer group in the United States. Statistics of twenty-two veterans a day taking their own lives mixes in my mind with the recent news that yet another of my own personal friends committed the act, making him the fifth in as many years. The article accomplishes two things. First, it offends the non-intended audience, startling them that someone would publicly say such a thing. Second, and more importantly, it frightens a handful of veterans close to the final act of desperation. The idea of being considered a coward by their peers, their friends, their brothers, terrifies them. Enough so to cause a few to reach out.

I spend the next five hours on a call with my friend, talking through his fears, while I simultaneously contact as many people as possible in the area to visit him at his home. By the end of our conversation, his voice is no longer heavy and frantic. He once again feels connected and cared for. He's still alive for fear of being thought a coward.

I arrive at a hostel called Jailhouse Accommodations. The old prison-turned-backpacker hostel is just a few miles from the airport. It's still too early to check in and go to my room. Typically, I'd take advantage of this time to explore my new surroundings and embrace the culture of a new nation. The combined emotional fatigue from our conversation and physical illness hits me like a truck, however. I fall asleep, upright, in a chair in the hostel's busy lobby until I'm allowed to check into my room. The thin, lumpy mattress and jagged springs are no match for my exhaustion. I continue where I left off for the next seventeen hours.

When I awake and check my email again, I see hundreds more vitriolic messages from people who've never tasted the cold metallic flavor of a gun barrel or felt the course fibrous rope of despair cinching taunt around their life force. The majority of which never struggled with depression, rather read about it in a book or on a Facebook update. Amid the volley of venom, a few other voices emerge. Ones long silenced by the overshadowing cries of their demons. Standing up for the first time as a result of those hard words, not the typical tiptoe approach they're accustomed to droning out. They open up to me.

I spend my next full day in New Zealand talking to veterans from the same place I was in just a few years ago. We speak about the tribulations associated with assimilation from war to the world. We discuss the difficulty in relationships and finding a job. The discomfort associated with visiting places we used to enjoy and having to look ourselves in the mirror everyday. Their fresh wounds open my old scars. In a café I never knew existed but always wanted to visit, I relive each of my most painful moments through their stories.

I think back to what Emerson wrote, a quote that until now, I disagreed with: *"Traveling is a fool's paradise. Our first journeys discover to us the indifference of places...I affect to be intoxicated with sights and suggestions, but I am not intoxicated. My giant goes with me wherever I go."*

Through all of my travels thus far, all of the nations, the people, the experiences, I unknowingly dragged this sadness. I laboriously shouldered the weight of the cumbersome giant of not just war, but the disconnect in which its return from created in me. The search for my place on earth and within humanity has perhaps, not been the physical one I have, for so many miles, believed. Perhaps it's more a sense of divine belonging, which we all unknowingly strive for.

The weight of that giant is somehow mitigated by the mutual connection and, in turn, assistance of my fellow man. Long periods of silent reflection mark the following hours and subsequent days. From Christchurch I board a bus headed for the small fishing town of Picton where I plan to take a five-hour ferry ride to the North Island capital city of Wellington.

The unrivaled splendor and magnificent beauty of the New Zealand countryside blurs in panoramic harmony with my thoughts as I stare out the bus window. Day cedes to night. Ours seems to be the only vehicle on the winding road. Fate chimes in through my headphones in the form of a City and Colour song. The lyrics mirroring my own emotions; the solitude of the endless highway, a constant struggle with internal demons, the chore of instilling hope despite personal feelings of hopeless, and ultimately, coming to the conclusion if one song could save a life, sing. Sing all you can sing.

We all have it. We all have an ability to sing in our own way. In a literal sense, I can't carry a tune for the life of me. And for the most part I, as an individual, have felt an overwhelming sense of hopelessness on even my brightest days; the weight of which could sink a ship. Yet, in the right moment, I still possess the ability to change the world for the better. We all have it, the magnanimous power to save the world, one impactful song, one kind word, one outstretched hand at a time.

My thoughts are rudely interrupted by the increasingly winding mountain road and the resulting tumult it has on my stomach. All of the poetic philosophical tirades dripping from my mind are wrung dry by the knotted chokehold my guts are in. The poor teenage athlete sitting next to me, no doubt returning home from boarding school for the weekend, is introduced to the half-digested contents of my stomach as I make the already musky-smelling bus slightly less pleasant to be in. Luckily the hat on my head a half a second ago secures the projectile emesis from being distributed any further. I'm now the least popular passenger on the double decker, superseding the grenade-like snoring tones emanating from seat 7b.

Well after dark, the winding road ends in the small fishing village of Picton. Making my apologies to anyone still willing to look me in the eye, I quickly move toward my big red backpack, now sitting on the curb. I make haste toward the only hostel in the town I can see. After the last forty-eight hours, my only desire is the solemn refuge of a thick blanket and a perfectly uneventful evening. Walking to my room and seeing two beautiful blonde European women in their mid-twenties hanging out with an overly-confident, early-twenty-something from Saudi Arabia is enough to peak my interest and shift my plans.

I drop off my bag in my room and return to the living room. Strategically, I position myself across from the trio's position in the communal area. Neither of the ladies seems terribly impressed with their present company. He brags about how much money his family has and asks the girls if they want to go to the bar.

"We want to see live music," says the shorter girl in a German accent. Her round face extenuates her big eyes. She seems to be the younger of the two. Twenty-three, I'd guess.

"What are you doing?" her friend asks me in a different accent. I can't place it. Scandinavian perhaps.

"Nothing really."

"Do you want to come to the bar with us?"

"Sure, let me grab my wallet."

Our unlikely foursome makes its way to the only street with enough lights to suggest anything could be happening. Two bars across from one another make up the scene in Picton. The ladies have to settle for the acoustic stylings of a sweaty, overweight gentlemen with a facial hair condition somewhere between a beard and a series of random hair patches glued to his cheeks.

Immediately upon entering, I confidently approach the bar and order a round. I return from the bar with a round of beers for the group. I distribute the pint glasses while the heavyset Kiwi on stage belts out an acoustic rendition of 3-6 Mafia that's nothing short of inspiring.

The young Saudi traveler repays me with a fist pump and shouts over the music, "You my nigga!" in a comically thick accent.

Looking startled, the tiny blonde German girl can't believe someone used such a word so freely.

"That is so bad to say," she exclaims.

"Yeah, it kind of depends," I reply.

"How? I thought it was very bad of a word."

"It can be, it depends on the amount of 'R' you use."

"What does that mean?"

"At the end of the word, if you use an 'A' sometimes it isn't as bad, but if you use an 'R' it is."

"I don't understand."

"But if you said it, it wouldn't be good no matter what. Same with me. We're not allowed to because we're white."

"What do you mean?"

"If you have dark skin you can get away with using the 'N' word. We're white so we can't use it at all. It's one of two off-limit words in the U.S."

She just stares at me through a set of confused doe-like eyes. To be honest, I'm the one explaining it and I'm confused. A word is a word isn't it? It's either bad or it isn't. The conversation turns to the second worse word in the U.S.

"What is the other one?" she asks in a thick German accent.

"The 'C' word."

"What word is that?"

"The 'C' word? Ohh, I'm not going to say that to you."

"Ohh, come on. What is it?"

"No way. There's no way I am going to teach you that word."

Tilting her head the way a child does when they aren't getting their way, she makes a final plea.

"Cunt. The 'C' word is cunt."

"What's that?"

"Nope. Not going there."

Turning to her Finnish friend she inquiries, "What is cunt?" The conversation between the tall Scandinavian and a guy who recently joined our group comes to an abrupt stop. I just look at her with shame in my eyes and shrug my shoulders like a twelve year old who just got caught teaching his little sister a bad word.

I attempt to explain, "In England, they use that word in similar frequency that you or I would use the word 'the.' It's just more culturally acceptable."

On a personal level, I'll never understand the pain and volatility associated with either of those words. Neither one has the ability to hurt me personally, yet on a certain level it still offends me when one person uses either to describe another person.

The word nigger can, in no way, cause physical harm to a person. No word can. Yet, it somehow cuts as deep as any knife. It conjures a notion of superiority of one human over another, representing the highest degree of intolerance. Despite this, some people use the word nigger in reference to a friend or someone close to them. In Australia last week, Luke called me, "A mad cunt," at least a dozen times. A term of endearment where he's from, but a terrible insult where I'm from.

So why do we do it? Why do we use a seemingly hate-filled word when speaking to a friend? Is it a way to communicate our friendship extends beyond the depths of that hate-filled expression? When the person who should be the most offended by the word uses it incessantly, is it an effort to rise above the hate of it? Possibly a way to dilute its potency? It can't be ignorance.

If we know enough about the history of a word to be offended that one person says it but not another, then we know enough to not use it at all. Racial, sexual, theological, gender, spiritual or cultural intolerance is an egregious stance to take against another human. Intolerance is the cornerstone of hate which has ignited almost every war in history.

To expect others to allow you to move through the world, opinion and belief in tact, without extending the same courtesy is the bedrock of discontent.

Tolerance and understanding. It seems terribly oversimplified. Imagine, if the next interaction you have with someone whose opinion is adjacent from your own that these pillars become the focal points of the exchange. Imagine what you can learn.

Personally, the above-mentioned words are not in rotation in my vernacular because I understand they cause distress. Other people don't feel the same as I do. I have to be tolerant of that. While I, in no way, condone or accept the hate associated with them, it's foolish to think these words will be removed from lexicon. Dropping the "N" word in casual conversation seems to be a sign of the times. Perhaps if people had more tolerance and understanding, they'd drop the "N" word from their vocabulary for good.

For the sake of our good time, we unwind the charged conversation in favor of humorous anecdotes about our collective traveling escapades. Probst. Skul. Salude. Cheers. We run the gambit on the selection of draft beers until the music and night fades.

The black coffee stains my teeth on its way to my churning gut. The boat labors through the bustling harbor on an otherwise perfect day. Marshmallow clouds lethargically pass over the top deck of the passenger ferry providing intermittent shade adding to the intense spinning feeling in my head; the result of being aggressively over-served last night.

I don't even remember returning to the hostel. Where does that compulsion come from? That thirst. It pulls at me like a puppeteer. No matter how many times I pay the lofty price the morning af-ter, I still find my way back in line. Waiving crumpled dollar bills at overworked bartenders. I don't regret it. Ever. I don't apologize for the behavior or protest any pride in it. I just sit in the fog of its aftermath. The churning, chaotic, wrenching, putrid physical state of paying the piper.

On our floating island, destined for the north half of New Zealand and the port city of Wellington, my attention divides between the assimilation of my closest friends from the comforts of war into the anarchy of civility and the physical suppression of releasing my breakfast over the railing.

A few hours later, I push my heavy legs off the boat and toward the city center. I find a cheap hostel room across the street from the train station I will depart from in the morning and think about sleeping. We're here, in this moment, once, and in it is where we should live. I change my shirt, lock my bag in the room and walk.

The golden woman steps with imaginative poetry, illuminating the hearts of foreign passersby. The percussive tones of street performers soundtrack the tempo of steps through now-crowded city streets. The faint whisper of salt hanging in the night air speaks softly to my olfactory nerve, completing the indulgent buffet of the senses.

In under an hour, Wellington becomes one of my favorite cities in the world without the pervasive accosting efforts others rely on to be memorable. It's subtle. The girl next door. For no reason exactly, I'm smitten with the unique curve of her smile and blue-collar grace.

And like the one perfect evening spent intertwined with another lonely traveler in Australia, our time together, this city and mine, is confined to the rise and fall of a single moon. The sun marks a moment of departure, and once again I turn my back and smile, satiated. The train carries me onward to Auckland. A hundred dollars takes me past more sheep than I've ever seen: Their pearlescent coats decorate the vast rolling green hills like the white caps of an endless emerald ocean's waves.

Eight hours into our twelve-hour journey the conductor announces to us that we will be stopping prematurely. A train has derailed ahead. It appears we will make the remainder of the trip by bus.

More than one patron vocalizes their complaint at the downgrade in accommodations. I just think about how lucky we are to have not been on the early train. Just as the sun sets on another day, we arrive in the crowded city bus station. Two blocks away a few hostels cater to backpackers such as myself.

I pay forty dollars for a room in the closest establishment to the depot. I sit alone amidst a group of travelers in the lobby area. It's the only place in the building with access to the Internet, as well as a group entertainment area where young men and women from a half a dozen different countries decide which movie to watch next.

After perhaps an hour of checking in with family and going over the stacks of unimportant emails in my inbox, I see two older men enter up the stairs and approach the front desk. Until now every other person here, including the guy behind the desk, is younger than I am by several years.

One of the men carries with him the weight of an arduous existence, tattered and stained by a life no doubt lived on the streets. The other man holds a fistful of money and attempts to secure a room for the homeless gentlemen for an evening.

The kid behind the counter takes no time to evaluate the status of the man.

"We're all full," he says, without any hesitation or compassion in his voice.

I know this isn't the case. When I paid for my room an hour ago, the very same person offered me my choice of rooms. Dejected, the unlikely pair shares a look of disbelief. The group of travelers stares conceitedly down their noses at the poor man.

I advance toward the two as they turn to depart and place my key in his filthy, trembling hand. "He can take my room then," I announce, in a way that's clearly not up for discussion to the putrid little shit now sinking behind the desk. I grab my bag and head out the door to anywhere, but here.

A hundred meters down the street I find similar domicile, rent a bed in a four-person room and make my way up to the third floor. Up until this point, I've had great luck renting four-person rooms. Typically, I haven't had to share them at all. I noticed immediately upon entering this room, however, that it's very occupied. Women's workout clothes hang from every possible location in an effort to dry post washing. Am I in a room with three females?

I place my giant red backpack in the small closet and head out into the evening, still frothing mad from the treatment the nameless man just endured. The streets of Auckland lack the whimsical charm of those in Wellington. The sidewalks are littered with a vagrant population, hands extended at knee level of unconcerned schools of human fish, navigating their own selfish streams.

I sit next to a young man, half covered by a sleeping bag. His name is Brian and has lived on the streets since running away from an abusive home five years ago. His eyes are sincere and he asks me for nothing. I spoil myself listening to his life's story. Slightly eccentric, yet perfectly suited for a movie script, I ask Brian, "Are you hungry?" and am not surprised by his answer.

I walk across the street to the all night pizza place, order a large-deluxe, meat special and personally deliver it to him, thanking him for sharing his amazing story. I repeat the process with Jimmy, and a man appropriately nicknamed "Stinky." Stinky's story is not as coherent as Brian's or Jimmy's, but his enthusiasm for Burger King more than makes up for the holes in his accounts of life on the streets.

The rising sun doesn't wake me. I sleep in past the chirping of the birds. It isn't until the first patrons of the park I slept in begin to stroll past my park bench bed, do my eyes flutter open. It's not in my capacity to explain why I chose to sleep unprotected under the countless stars in the middle of a strange city. Perhaps something as simple and visceral as the piercing feeling of frailty and stinging cold of the night air invigorates a connection with the moments we're all so close to. We are all one mistake away from a park bench home. Those who call this place their residence are no more or less human than you or I.

I explore the park, the city museum, the street art and the pulse of hustle that is the city's heartbeat. Continuing the theme from last night, I have breakfast with Darrelle, and lunch with Susan, marveling in their accounts.

For hours, I sit and observe countless people walk past a piece of beautiful artwork at the intersection of two of the city's busiest streets. Not one person looks up to take it in for over an hour and a half. A woman in her mid-twenties stops. She removes her headphones and halts like a large rock tossed into a steadily moving river. And just like that, the current around her shifts.

A man in a business suit stops behind her. A young Asian couple sees the two looking at the statue and pulls a camera from a small bag and takes a photo. Two more people stop to appreciate what's been there the entire time, previously unnoticed. As unceremoniously as she stopped, the young blonde woman places the tiny white earbud back in place and steps forward, removing the stream's obstruction. With her go the others. For two more hours I sit, watching thousands of busy bodies pass by, not one looks up. Heads down, feet fast, rushing to the next part of life without taking the moment to live.

My day continues, and I make a second trip to the ATM for more cash. To my estimate, I've purchased somewhere around five hundred dollars worth of meals in the last twenty-four hours. By nightfall I sit alone in a small pub, making friends with each successive pint of stout, feeling no commonality with the affluent patrons of the establishment. People suffer while others celebrate. That's the nature of things. Is there a solution for that? If so, it's likely beyond my limited intellect to decipher. Perhaps giving a fuck is a good place to start.

I'm not entirely sure if I do or not. Give a fuck that is. If I did, I wouldn't be sucking back a nine-dollar drink every fifteen minutes.

I'd give that to someone who needs it, right? I don't feel bad, just out of place. Out of rhythm with other people. Cognitive juxtapose of empathy for and complete dissociation with the ethos of my fellow man rises and recedes like the contents of my glass. How sophomoric to recognize the idiosyncrasies, which create division in your species, yet not have the capacity to affect them indefinitely.

My flight is set to depart for Fiji at 9 a.m. It looks like it's a little before three. My vision is blurry and my wallet is empty. I haven't been back to the room where I left my bag yesterday.

After a few missed turns, I find the hostel once again, make my way up the stairs and fumble my way into the dorm-style room. It's dark and I'm drunk. I bring a herd of elephants with me through the door, awakening the room's other occupant. I apologize profusely and she responds in a thick French accent, "It's okay. Is that red bag yours? I didn't think you were coming back."

I settle into the bottom bunk next to hers and we begin to converse in the darkness. Her name is Tiffany. Of French Polynesian descent, she's worked as a maid in New Zealand for several months, trying to secure a permanent residency.

We exchange travel stories. I'm surprised by her candor as she discusses previous relationships, as well as a miscarriage she had the previous summer.

It takes me partially by surprise when we begin to kiss. She's still in her bunk and I in mine, but not for long. Soon she crawls into the already cramped confines of my twin bunk bed and our interaction amplifies as all four hands explore and legs intermingle.

She utters a phrase I've heard before, one that always ends up being a lie, "We're not having sex, just so you know."

Thirty minutes later we're both covered in bodily fluids and I check the time. I have to get on a bus to the airport in forty minutes. I set my alarm for fifteen minutes from now. Sleep for fourteen of them. Roll out of the sticky bed and into the shower directly across the hallway. The steam from the shower immediately fills the tiny closet-like room. The toilets and sinks are located down the hall.

Still drunk, I step into the jetstream of near-scalding water and begin what needs to be a very quick shower. As though someone cut an elevator cable containing the digested contents of all of the meals and stout black beers of the past twenty-four hours, my guts drop hard and fast into my colon. I'm not sure how many people are familiar with the term "Guinness shits," but I assure you, they're real and not something to be taken lightly.

I'm covered in both soap and shampoo, soaking wet and naked. Time ticks like a suitcase bomb, ready to detonate. I take a mental note of how far the toilet is. Too far. I'll never make it. Panic sets in. I'm hyperventilating. Terror-induced adrenaline surges through each capillary. I look to my feet where the waffle-shaped drain cover easily allows the water to escape. I'm sure it goes to the same place as the toilets down the hall.

I'm not proud of it, but I make the decision that must be made. An object the size, shape and consistency of a human brain exits my body like a paratrooper from the back of a cargo plane and lands with an audible splat on the mosaic tile at my feet.

Instantly, the abundant heavy steam molecules bind with the recently introduced fecal particles, producing something that, I can only assume, smells exactly like Satan's morning breath. I gag and watch in horror as the waffle drain cover prevents the semi-solid pile of human excrement from escaping the hot foggy environment. It must be done. I have to man up and get this accomplished. I feel the ingredients from each of my previous meals compress and squeeze through the void between my toes as I attempt to stomp that massive heap of shit down the waffle-shaped drain cover. Again and again, I repeat the process. It takes only a few minutes of my morning, but assuredly takes several years off my life.

After spending an additional five minutes scrubbing the bottom of my foot, I towel off and head back across the hall where Tiffany now lies passed out. I put on my dirty jeans and t-shirt, pick up my bag, give her a swift smack on the ass and make my way to the street. Today I'm going to Fiji. ❀

CHAPTER TWENTY

The Mind's Island

*"The future is meant for those who are willing to let go of
the worst parts of the past."*—Corey Taylor

Some people dream about a trip to the exotic island destination of
Fiji. The picturesque sunsets, the pristine white sand beaches and
local culture. I'm not one of those people. My experience in Fiji is the
combination of three equally, unimportant factors.

First of all, it's actually cheaper to have a one-day layover in Fiji
than to fly directly to Hawaii where I'm meeting with a good friend.
Secondly, my father always wanted to visit the island. Knowing I always wanted to visit Thailand, he was not shy about rubbing it in my
face that he traveled to the Southeast Asian country before I did.
Hence, I want to "beat" him to Fiji. I fully understand how child-
ish this is, but that's the nature of our relationship. Lastly, and most
important to me, I want to drink the water to see if it tastes anything
like the overpriced crap they put in the Fiji Water bottles in the States.

I hire a guy at the airport to drive me around for the day at a cost
of under a hundred dollars. Despite explicitly telling him I want to go
to where the locals eat and see parts of the town typically not visited

by tourists, he repeatedly takes me to nothing but cheesy tourist destinations. An overpriced hot springs, a whorishly decorated temple and a beachside resort featuring overpriced beers and umbrella drinks.

The highlight of my experience on the island is driving by three separate impromptu games of football played by local barefoot children and adults alike. From the road, passing by, I easily see each of the participants' teeth displayed through vibrant, genuine smiles. Having nothing and everything all at once.

Nathan and Angela graciously permit me to spread the contents of my nomadic lifestyle over their living room floor for a week.

The history, which Nathan and I share, is something analogous to brothers. A decade earlier, we served together as Army Rangers in Iraq and Afghanistan. We stood and fought together side by side in the streets of Tikrit, as well as Columbus, Georgia.

After the military, Nathan was an integral part of my civilian assimilation. We both struggled in our own ways with the transition from the special operations lifestyle. Nathan thrived in the chaos of war, it was only natural that he'd continue to pursue those endeavors after his time in service. He spent close to a decade working as a communications specialist in various war-torn, third-world countries. He seems different to me this time around, however, some disposition in him I can't quite place.

The reprieve of halting in Hawaii with family following such a whirlwind movement around the world supersedes even the natural beauty of the island. We spend the week laughing at the foolishness and futility of our youth.

The three of us spend each afternoon embarking on little island adventures, hiking, snorkeling and scouring farmer's markets for the perfect ingredients to make dinner with.

We reminisce in the smoke of his BBQ grill on his porch, overlooking the splendor of the Pacific Ocean, pressing into the Hawaiian shoreline. That's when it hits me, what's changed in him. He's happy. He found someone who compliments his goofy aggression and calms his Viking heart.

In our twenties, Nathan was a junkyard dog, viciously loyal and not the beast you ever wanted to be on the receiving end of. The thing is, watching him now, laughing and smiling, he's still just as dangerous. Angela just brought him inside, effectively settling something in him. It's altogether impressive and baffling how the presence of the right woman impacts a warrior's outward temperament.

I catch a momentary glimpse of my old friend's previous self when a drunken neighbor insults Angela. I'd personally witnessed Nathan, single-handedly, take on and render unconscious four attackers at once. To say this man stands absolutely no chance of defeating Nathan in this form of melee is an understatement. Nathan knows this and responds calmly. I see maturation unfold before me. He no longer feels the need to prove himself. Despite the incessant taunting by the drunken neighbor, Nathan refuses to dismantle him.

There's a dividing line between men and boys. It isn't the length of a beard, or size of displayed muscle, or ability to fornicate with slews of women. Rather, when the scale tips and you've fought enough battles to know the difference between necessary conflict and an attempt to prove yourself. A man proven in combat has no need to confirm himself in any other arena. All other crucibles are, by comparison, moot.

Nathan and Angela and I settle back into our beers and enjoy the sunset. Hawaii becomes the forty-seventh state of fifty in the U.S. where I've consumed a beer. The only three left are Alaska and North and South Dakota. In my final days in Hawaii, I hatch a plan to fly to Alaska, purchase a vehicle and drive to the other two, completing my long-running quest.

Nathan and I wish each other well as he and Angela drop me off at the airport, both of us knowing we're too much like family to worry about parting. We both know we'll be in one another's presence again. The goodbye is short and appropriate for two aging soldiers.

I take my first domestic flight in over a year. Traveling from one U.S. state to another is more complicated than any international travel I've done to date. The process created by the TSA is enough to make even the most tranquil passenger grind their teeth flat. In a country I fought for, I'm assumed a criminal and treated as such. To date, the intrusive actions of the TSA have resulted in the capture of zero terrorists, have cost taxpayers billions of dollars, countless hours and infinite headaches. A giant play, the illusion of safety and a false sense of authority bestowed upon those lacking the mental faculty to comprehend the consequences of their actions. All in the name of perceived security. We pay an extra tax to have our freedoms systematically removed, applauding. The artwork of social conditioning on display in the form of serpentine lines and confiscated fingernail clippers.

I digress. ✦

CHAPTER TWENTY-ONE

Alaska

"There is nothing noble in being superior to your fellow man; true nobility is being superior to your former self."—Ernest Hemingway

The wheels punch the tarmac with just enough commotion to jar me awake. The blue haze of early morning ominously lingers in the Alaskan air around the Anchorage airport. There's no customs check this time. A seven-hour flight over the ocean, landing over five thousand miles from where I was born and I'm still in my own country. I can hardly remember the last time I flew on a domestic flight.

I sit at the only open establishment enjoying a large coffee and chocolate chip muffin. Just to make things interesting, I decide to give myself only twenty-four hours to find and buy the vehicle I will drive to South Dakota. A van seems like a logical choice given the amount of room, and allowing me to cook and sleep inside. Sifting through various online ads, I begin emailing sellers from the terminal. Ideally, I need to find someone able and willing to pick me up in the vehicle I'll buy, then drop them off and be on my way.

I quickly find three potential matches for the journey ahead. Each has a bed in them already. It's mid-morning before anyone messages me back. I decide that getting to the city center will make it easier for me to withdraw money and test drive each. As I wait for the bus, cold spastic raindrops break upon my shoulders. An interesting climatic variation from the consistent beams of comforting sunlight that fell from the Hawaiian sun less than a day before.

The bus delivers me directly in front of my bank. As the bank teller counts out the stack of hundred-dollar bills, she politely asks, "What do you plan to do with your savings?"

"Cocaine and hookers," I reply, my thick beard half covers my wicked grin. She lets out an awkward giggle unsure if I'm joking. "Lots of cocaine and hookers," I continue. Her laughter, along with any hope at future eye contact vanishes.

I shove the envelope into my pant pocket and walk back out into the inconsistent drizzle of the grey Anchorage morning. Sitting on the curb, I wait for the first of the three sellers to arrive. *He's late. I hate dealing with people from Craigslist.* I think to myself, checking the time for the third time in five minutes.

The bank security guard monitors me, walking past my position on the curb several times. After the third pass he finally asks, "What are you doing?"

"Just waiting for my hookers and cocaine to show up. What are you into, mate?"

Perplexed at the candid response, the look on his face gives tell to his youth and innocence. "I'm just waiting to test drive a car from Craigslist," I continue to avoid having the real police called on me.

"Ohh, okay. That makes sense. You from around here?"

"Nope, just flew in from Hawaii a couple of hours ago."

"Ohh, you're from Hawaii then?"

"Nope, I flew there from New Zealand."

"Are you from New Zealand?"

"Nope. It was just one of the twenty-six countries I've traveled through this year."

"What? Why?"

"Why not?"

"Do you travel for work?"

"No, I travel for life. I travel because it makes me happy. Right now I've given myself twenty-four hours to find and buy a vehicle and start driving south."

"That sounds crazy to me. Why would you want to do that?"

I think for a moment. I think about what crazy is. A flash of images cycles through my mind in an instant. Images of people afraid to venture beyond the comfort of their couch. I think about the constant barrage of fear-based media in my country, subconsciously repeating to citizens that the world is a dangerous place. The status quo has become my nemesis.

Without explanation, I respond, "I'm willing to find out what impossible means."

His eyes rock back and forth, trying to find meaning in what I just said. A frumpy-looking man in ill-fitting clothing hops out of a dilapidated, red Astro van, interrupting our conversation. He introduces himself in what sounds like a thick Eastern European accent. I can't even make out his name. The van he arrives in is not the same year or even the same color as the one in his ad. As if I wasn't going to notice.

"You want to test drive?"

What in the fuck? Not this piece of shit, I think to myself. The look on my face expresses the same sentiment.

"I have two vans. This one and the one in the ad. They are both for sale. This one, I can sell to you for two thousand. The other is four thousand, five hundred. So this one is less."

Yeah, no shit. He didn't even attempt to clean it out. The inside looks worse than my first apartment after a keg party. I can tell just sitting in the passenger seat that it runs like a two-legged dog. This shit sled wouldn't make it out of Alaska.

"Let's see the other one," I insist, as we pull out of the parking lot.

Just getting to the second van is a hassle, which is parked in a storage yard he doesn't even have a key for. A friend of his meets us there, leaving us to the fine art of awkward conversation. He continues to talk up both vehicles in the kind of sheisty way that makes you want to take a shower.

The second van is in slightly better condition, but appraises at $2,500, not the $4,500 he's asking. The windshield is cracked and the stereo is missing. After a short test drive, I pull into a gas station close to the bank to discuss the price. I offer five hundred over the blue book value, but he just laughs. "I just spent two thousand dollars to have the steering fixed and I won't take less than the asking price."

"That's your problem. The van is only worth $2,500 and I'm offering you $3,000 cash right now."

"No, you see it's worth $2,500, but I spent $2,000 on it, so I have to get $4,500 or I lose money."

"That doesn't make sense. If I buy it for $4,500 and turn around and try to sell it tomorrow, I'd only get $2,500 for it."

"Well, that is your problem, not mine."

Is this guy serious? This guy is serious. I make one last attempt to offer him the three grand. He just says that his friend told him the vehicle is worth six thousand and so really he's losing $1,500 by selling it for $4,500.

My brain feels like it's being struck by a hammer every time he opens his mouth. I can't take it anymore. In as polite of a tone I can manage in my utterly confused state, I mutter, "Good luck with that." I turn and walk away.

An hour later, a maroon Dodge 2500 van identical to the pictures I scanned over online pulls into the parking lot I'm sitting in. I like this beast instantly. It has brand new carpet, tires, shocks, cabinets, windshield and mattress. It's perfect. I haven't been behind the wheel since Australia and haven't driven on the right side of the road in months. It's the ideal vehicle for the next phase of travel. The only problem is, it's priced three hundred dollars over the budget limit I set for myself, and the seller isn't budging.

I tell him I have one more van to test drive and will get back to him before the end of my twenty-four hour purchase window. In the middle of the test drive a good friend sees I'm in Anchorage via a social media post. He messages me saying his sister lives here and already agreed to pick me up, and let me stay at her place for the evening. I walk across the parking lot and into the grocery store to find something small to eat while I wait for her.

I drop the cumbersome pack to my side, remove my faded ball cap, wiping the sweat from my forehead. The overcast morning blossoms into the vibrant heat of the mid-afternoon. Tossing the hat at my feet, propped against my faithful red bag, I watch people walk by the store entrance, and enjoy the meager package of lunch meat I just purchased.

Not more than a minute later a man, avoiding eye contact, tosses three coins into my hat as he enters the store. What in the fuck... Attempting to make sense of it, scratching my nearly-mange, six-inch beard, I look down at my tattered clothes, then at my weathered pack. *Holy shit! He thinks I'm homeless! Well, I guess he's right. I mean, I AM homeless.* I shrug my shoulders, more confused than offended.

It takes me a few seconds to truly appreciate the irony of the situation. I have fifty crisp one hundred dollar bills in an envelope in my left pant pocket. I have a laptop, an iPad and a smart phone in my bag along with a solar panel charger to keep them running as I traverse the world. Without much more than a passing glance, this man seemingly reduces my role in society to beggar.

Judging a person based on appearance is a terrible habit we're all guilty of. To an extent, there's a programmed antipathy toward the homeless in our society. If you're poor, you must be lazy. If you're lazy, you're a drain on society, and in turn, you're a drain on me. Sure,

I'll toss you loose change, because doing so provides me with a moral high ground. It makes me feel better.

Can you blame people, really? What if you or I attempt to take on the plight of every disadvantaged human we encounter? What will that do to you? What a drain created on your otherwise merry day. After all, most homeless people are addicts anyway, right? They just use that money for drugs or alcohol. Any help you provide will likely be squandered. It's best if we simply build shelters for them to keep them away from our walled communities and dignified family shopping centers.

The fact most individuals seem to miss is how close they are to a similar fate. One illness, one injury, one unforeseen incident and the wheels of fate can slam your ride into reverse. You are, at any given time, a single incident from being on the street. You are, at your core, no better or worse than the dirt-stained man you avoid eye contact with on your way to church.

Seventy-five cents...cheapskate.

I notice the shiny red, sport utility vehicle roll slowly to the curb where I sit, and internally debate the social obligation to provide for those with less than myself. I'm haggard, completely haggard, making my identification easy enough. Nick's sister makes good on her promise to take in his transient friend. She feeds me, buys me my Alaskan beer and shows me to a lavish guest bedroom in her and her husband's home.

I message the seller of the Dodge van before the sun rises the next morning, meet with him and purchase my new home for $5,000 cash, exactly twenty-three hours after landing in Alaska. This act shifts not only my living condition, but, my life condition. I've been eastbound once around the spinning blue ball. I've been, for the most part alone in my experience.

The dawn of a new direction beams through my windshield. A strong southern pull draws me to a new series of human interactions and irrevocable growth. A gravitational shift of polarity tilts my world from its current spin, southward. My world maintains its status as a shiny round metal object in the pinball machine of life.

The vibrant beams of golden sun piercing the windshield slowly give way to an angry, spitting cloud. The sheer majesty of the Alaskan landscape is so altogether captivating that I nearly miss the young man standing at the first intersection I roll through in over an hour. In the universal, 'can I get a ride' gesture, the lanky hitchhiker displays his thumb beacon in hopes of landing a lift.

"Thank you so much," he exclaims with a heavy eastern European accent through a wide-face grin.

"Yeah, no worries bud. Where are you heading?"

"I go to marker 146."

"I'm not sure what that means."

"It's this way. On this road. You just keep going. Where are you going to?"

"South."

"This is a cool van."

"Thank you! I just bought it today."

Over the next hour we get familiar with one another's backstory. Ivan is only twenty years old but has tried to become an American citizen for the past two years. He grew up in the draconian Belarusian regime. His enthusiasm for traveling and life is palpable in every word he utters. He didn't grow up with the same freedom of movement that so many in the U.S. take for granted. He cherishes every minute he spends in the United States, but desires to see the entire world. After explaining to him where I've been and where I hope to go, Ivan becomes, quite possibly, more excited for my adventure than even I am. "Ohh boy!" he repeats in a thick Russian accent.

Driving forty miles past where I intended on stopping for the evening, I drop Ivan at the front door of the camp where he lives. A few miles earlier, we passed by an amazing raging river, lined with giant boulders. Redirecting 180 degrees, I set out determined to have the first morning in my new home be as scenic as possible. I now have a malleable front porch view, one fully equipped with the autonomy to change to fit my desire. Through the pitch-black Alaskan darkness I strain my eyes searching for the half-hidden turnoff. The oversized tires find dirt for the first time under my ownership and I slowly pull the red beast to a halt, unsure if the earth will drop off into the audibly raging river below.

The cornucopia of shining skyward diamonds illuminates a new-found utopia in my heart. The vastness, the incomprehensible vastness of that night sky, untainted by the fluorescent flicker of man's bastardized contribution to light, explodes with greater tenacity, grace and endless shimmer than the totality of all the world's fireworks. Never has a sleep occurred so sound.

The crack of first light crests the glacier feeding my liquid stereo. Eyes flutter awake to a new world of possibility and endless potential. Without the constraints of deadline, I reach slowly for the book sitting open next to my bed. The brisk night air left a thin layer of ice crystals on the interior window, making the grey fleece blanket all the more enjoyable.

I break free momentarily from my swaddle to fire up one of the two gas-powered burners, which make up the bulk of my kitchen. Along with the small camping grill, I purchased a cast iron skillet, one pot, a pair of red bowls and plates, two forks, knives and spoons, a percolator, a can opener, a spatula and one very necessary blue tin coffee cup. A meager set of belongings by the account of most of my peers. However, the ability to roll out of bed and make myself coffee has me feeling like royalty.

The heat radiating off my new blue tin cup warms my hands as I sit on a large stone admiring my new front yard. The boulders to my right scream for me to come climb them in the way a new piece of playground equipment yells to a young child through the window of their third period math class. I resist the urge to forego the utter serenity of the moment. The dopamine surge contracts my heart with ferocity. Perhaps, it's the coffee.

I spend the morning giving in to my child-like tendencies and pulling on every rock in eyesight, then find rubber to road once more. With nowhere to go and a lifetime to get there, I hammer the pedal through some of the most heavenly terrain on earth. Four-hundred-and-fifty miles in a single day and across the first of many international border crossings to be made in the fifteen-year-old Dodge. The unique cutout, twenty meters wide, of the thickest coniferous skyscrapers I've ever seen marks the divide between another new country and my own. Yukon, Canada.

South. South. South. Something sucks me south. It's impossible to explain. Despite falling quickly in love with my present surroundings, my desire to move through exceeds the will to indulge. South.

In under thirty-six hours I see a whitetail fox, two moose, a beluga whale and a very unimposing black bear. The cheap antenna struggles valiantly, but can't seem to find a station. I haven't seen another car, in either direction, for over an hour. The Yukon of Northern Canada is a world in and of itself. Despite the unique expansive wonderland of endless pines and unique wildlife, something of a magnetic pull draws me away. With all this recent movement, any stagnation, even for a day, feels uncomfortable.

The long stretches of silent road begin to take their toll on my psyche. To stay awake, I begin reciting the little bit of Shakespeare I know from heart. Hundreds of miles from where I dropped off the last hitchhiker, I see a thin man in a denim jacket walking along the empty road with a noticeable limp.

"You need a ride, bud?"

A sort of mumbled acceptance of the offer accompanies a slight nod of the head as the man of Native descent laboriously climbs into the cab of my van. My hopes for a little conversation in return for the ride gradually slip away. Sitting, rocking back and forth, clenching his silver coffee travel mug, muttering incoherently to himself. A half an hour into our time together he blurts out the question, "You ever pan for gold in Nevada?"

An exceptionally random, yet specific question, I think to myself. "Do the tables in Vegas count?" I respond with a chuckle. "Sorry, different kind of gold," I continue in an effort to not come across as mocking the obviously troubled man.

"All kinds of gold," he returns, "the world runs on gold. Money is evil, but we need it to keep the world moving. The gas in this van that picked me up was bought with money. Money makes the world turn. It's evil, but it makes the world turn."

After what is one of the most random, poignant, pragmatic statements I've heard in sometime, the man goes back to his incoherent ramblings, leaving me in a state of disbelief.

Another hour and a half of spastic dialog and excessive fidgeting from my travel mate and something in the steering starts to feel off. An out-of-place sound and minor vibration quickly transforms into a chaotic dissonance and a pungent-burning odor. The wheel in my hands violently fights against me as I attempt to keep the van straight. A brief glance to the rearview and I notice the rear tire decided to free itself from the steel rim. That sinking feeling grabs ahold of my stomach and pulls it south as I realize I never checked to see if the van had a spare tire.

We're a hundred miles from nowhere and haven't seen another vehicle moving in either direction for at least a half an hour. I remember my old Dodge pickup truck had a spare affixed to the undercarriage near the rear axle.

The breath returns to my lungs like surfacing from moments underwater as I discover that beautiful hunk of emergency rubber sleeping safely under the van. The minor inconvenience is a chance to get to know my passenger a little better. As I begin lifting the rear end with the jack, he removes the lug nuts and says, "It wasn't far from here, no not far at all."

"What wasn't far from here?"

"Where it happened. The accident."

"What happened?"

"I was thrown from the car my cousin was driving. He was drunk. Flying too high. Hit the pole. Spent eleven months in a full body cast. Just got it off a couple of weeks ago. He's dead." The man lifts his shirt to show the miracles of modern medicine displayed by a series of impressive surgical scars. "That's why I got to get to Whitehorse, got my follow-up doctor's appointment this afternoon."

"Holy shit! What if no one picked you up?"

"I would have had to walk."

"But that's over two-hundred miles and I don't mean to sound like a mom here, but you're in no condition to be walking two hundred meters, let alone miles!"

"Don't have no choice. Don't have no car and no hospital where I live."

There's no self-pity in his voice. No entitlement or blame exists either. It's evident he is by far from being a man of means. He has little left in the world, but he is alive, a fact he seems truly grateful for.

For the remainder of the drive into the provincial capital I can't help but be in awe of this man, I feel proud to know him, if only for a few hours.

Just shy of the hospital he points at a corner gas station, signaling for me to pull over. "Gotta get me my coffea. Love my coffea! Doctors tell me not to drink it, but I love me coffea!"

I want to hop out and buy it for him. I want to buy him a full meal and drive him the rest of the way to the hospital, but he refuses, just saying we made good time and he can make it from here. Still clenching his small dented thermos, he passes a sincere thank you and climbs out of the van. A testament to the spirit of human resilience.

A quick stop at a small tire shop brings to my attention the elevated cost of goods and services this far north. For someone on a fixed travelers income, paying twice as much for a spare tire is a hell of a kick, one that somehow, however, doesn't sting as much as it should have. After a few hours with my last passenger, I'm exceedingly thankful for my ability to hop in and out of the big van without the inhibition of pain. I'm thankful that even though it isn't in my budget, I have the resources available to replace the brand new tire, which shredded off the rim like the lid of a tin can when exposed to an electric can opener.

I am, more than anything, and above all else, thankful that in this moment I'm alive and I'm free. Free to move in any direction and at any pace my soul burns for; free to breathe as deeply, the same air whose crisp inertia has fed my well-being since the day of my birth, yet so often flowed without its due appreciation. I'm free to be the way in which we're all free to be, every one of us, it's just taken me this long to fully understand that it's been my choice all along. A bird's eye view is often necessary to beat life's labyrinth. For now, I'm soaring. ✤

CHAPTER TWENTY-TWO

South

"Never regret thy fall, O Icarus of the fearless flight. For the greatest tragedy of them all is never to feel the burning light."—Oscar Wilde

A substantial portion of the major highway through the Yukon is a dirt road. More moose than men from here to there. More wild than tame. More nature than precision-placed plastic and concrete. The old paper map I acquired at the border crossing brings me back to a simpler time before a palm-held electronic device pinpointed my location to within a meter.

Overlooking the pristine lake sitting in the pocket of the surrounding mountains, my hands and feet regain warmth by the flicker of the first fire I've built in years. As a boy camping under the stars and cooking over an open flame was somewhat commonplace. As an adult, however, I'd grown so far from the comfort of simplicity and all of its cathartic side effects. The cast iron skillet erupts euphorically as the Brussels sprouts and bacon simmer in a symphony of synchronized sizzle and smell.

I'm enamored by it. Obsessed. The harmony of its dance speaks to me, softly at first, then with a throaty crack. The essence of the flame moves through me, much in the way the waves have. These two elements intertwine with my soul, the extremities of existence.

It's just a patch of land, but it pulses with the energy of generations of men who still sustain their families with the fish in this lake and the beasts that roam these back dropping mountains. An unexpected, yet, welcome return to primal. A reminder of where we all came from and how far we've come, for good or bad, since living off the land was the rule rather than the exception.

The desolate road begins to bend and slither up a series of mountain passes as the van now named "Falcor" rumbles through the Northern Rocky Mountains. Different than their Colorado counterpart, but very much the same. Entering British Colombia feels a little familiar. The wildlife is just as present as more caribou, bison and black bear show themselves in a lazy sort of fashion. The mountains give way to the flat lands of Alberta and a relative return to society. The series of paved roads and electronic signs advertising unnecessary products overwhelm my senses.

For the first time since purchasing the van, I'm relocated to parking its tires on concrete for the evening. A roadside rest station provides temporary domicile for an evening. The reality that not every night on this trip will be spent in a picturesque location doesn't detract from my excitement. An odd longing for a place I just left a few hours prior festers in my gut.

The way it does on long drives, the road rolls under the rubber. The miles past, and my mind drifts from one thought to the next until entire worlds are created in my imagination, and then annihilated by the act of stopping again for gas. Two dollars a gallon isn't a bad price, but the cost is for a liter. My ability to convert is getting better. Multiply by four and subtract a little bit. That means, I'm paying closer to seven dollars a gallon. The cost savings of not paying rent and cooking over a fire is offset by driving hundreds of miles in a vehicle that averages about 18 miles to the gallon. (Conversion: 7.7 kilometers to the liter.)

Early one morning a discomfort wakes me before the rising of the sun. I'm cold, but that isn't it. I've been still for a few hours, but feel an untamable need to flow. Flick of the key and the engine fires with impeccable reliability. East now. More east, than south, in my direction. I'm hungry, but don't want to stop. Something has a hold on me. As if the road needs my presence, I push the pedal to sooth my need for new surroundings. Within the hour, and still before the rising sun sees fit to show itself, I notice a man on the side of the major highway.

The other cars zip past him at seventy miles an hour. Somehow I see him, propped up by a wooden cane and with a small pack slung over his right shoulder. Pulling over as far off the road as I can, I'm at least a quarter of a mile past him before I bring the van to a full stop from the speed I was maintaining.

"Sorry about that." I apologize as he climbs in. "I didn't mean to make you run that far."

"Ohh, it's no hassle, I'm just glad that someone stopped. I'm actually kind of surprised you did. Most people won't stop on the highway like that."

His name is Greydon. He carries a noticeable exhaustion in his eyes. He tells me he attempted to sleep in a truck stop the night before, but was kicked out. The night prior to that he tried to sleep on a bench, but feared he'd freeze to death if he didn't get up and move around throughout the night. Faded and leathered by a life on the road, his arms are covered in the quality-type tattoos you get in prison or from a friend just starting the skilled art who needs practice.

His story of being on the road since sixteen years old is frequently interrupted as he, mid-sentence, falls into a deep sleep, immediately snoring as though he'd been asleep for hours. This happens multiple times over our three hundred miles together. He tells me tales of learning the craft of working on an oil rig at seventeen and lying about his age to get the job. About the first trucker who picked him up and warned him of life on the road and all of its hardships. He tells of his time hanging out with the notorious motorcycle club, The Hells Angels, and the son he has, but has never met.

I can't help but think that if Christopher McCandless of *Into the Wild* had survived Alaska, his story may not have been so romanticized, but rather fizzled into a tale closer to that of my narcoleptic passenger. Or perhaps, he'd have capitulated and returned to the commercial comfort of his past. Or maybe, just maybe he'd go on to eloquently express the need for long lost human experience and pursuit of a primal freedom buried under our material comforts.

Similar to the aboriginal passenger I helped get to his hospital appointment, this man has no self pity in his voice. He is free, not always comfortable, but he's free.

We stop at a roadside diner where I offer to buy breakfast. I relish the opportunity to listen to his life's story. A greasy dive restaurant by most of my peer's standards, Graydon's eyes double in size as he sees the prices on the menu. "You could buy two dozen eggs for that price!" he exclaims, as he flips through the omelet options on page two. His perspective is refreshing.

It's the first meal served to me since leaving Anchorage, and in that time I've begun to appreciate the gap between the cost of comfort and its value. Simultaneously, I feel privileged to buy breakfast for a hungry man and ashamed the small amount I spend could be better spent purchasing food for a group of those in need.

We box up the leftovers and return to the road. I take Graydon all the way to Saskatoon, Saskatchewan. As we part and without prompting, Graydon says, "I know I didn't thank you for picking me up and for buying me breakfast. Please don't take that as me being ungrateful. I know you're supposed to say thank you when someone does something kind for you. I appreciate it. I'm not entirely used to it, but I appreciate it."

I wish him well before making a hard right turn to the south. Toward the U.S. border with renewed perspective, and toward the last two remaining states in my home country where I have yet to drink a beer.

A torrid stretch of endless asphalt atop an expansive sea of dirt. The hum of four over-inflated, all-terrain tires joins the symphonic buzz of the rushing breeze through the manually lowered window. The patch of dirt I advance through is strikingly similar to the last hundred kilometers. So much so that had I not just engaged in a short conversation with the single border patrol agent at the shack-like checkpoint, I wouldn't even know I transcended yet another international border.

What a strange concept those seemingly arbitrary lines in the soil become at this stage in my journey. Where once nomadic tribes occupied undefined regions, we have, in recent years, created a series of lines which we must have permission to draw outside of. Human beings, the most advanced species on earth, must now ask permission to travel. You must pay for and obtain a document and answer a series of questions to walk from one patch of dirt to another.

There's no doubt an inverse relationship between freedom and safety. The perpetual looming perceived threat masterfully delivered by the media that some foreign bad guy who speaks a different language and holds a different set of religious beliefs infiltrating and creating terror among our innocent civilians seems to be enough to create an obsequious populace. So freedom is surrendered in the name of safety.

Back in the land of the free, I return my passport to the secret compartment under my console and note the shifting in distance markers to miles. After just five of them I begin to miss kilometers, they pass by so much faster than miles. As the sun fades in the distant horizon, I roll into the town of Williston, North Dakota. While I wouldn't describe the place as sleepy, I also wouldn't call it bustling. A burrito and beer are long overdue at this point. Sitting alone in the back corner of 3 Amigos Southwest Grill, I check off state 49 of 50 on my list, finish my foil wrapped meal, and move on.

Day capitulates to the tenebrous evening and, like so many nights before, I have no plan for where I'll sleep tonight. The heavy, hazy sensation of cramming for a midterm exam creeps up and grabs my eyes. Refusing to surrender, I push further south, actively searching for a place to call home for the night.

The lights of the small town up ahead would otherwise be a promising site, except stealth camping (a cool way of saying "sleeping in your car") is made more difficult in populated areas. Passing by, I observe a small local tavern.

Up until this point, I've avoided staying overnight in parking lots. The thought now occurs to me, however, that this could actually be the perfect place. Bars are the one type of establishment accustomed to people leaving their vehicles overnight after having a few too many libations.

With the exception of a small exodus of patrons stumbling by around the last call hour, I go undisturbed for the evening. Waking just before the sun, I opt to start moving south in lieu of eating breakfast. Twenty minutes into my drive the sight to my right is more than I can take in while driving. A gorgeous landscape. That line of golden mesas set the backdrop and trap an ominous looming fog layer, settling over a winding mystic river with sporadic patches of giant lush coniferous trees in the foreground. I stop and drink from the moment.

The small, two-burner stove brings the kettle to boil as the bacon and eggs sizzle in the cast iron skillet in my instant roadside diner. Almost as if cued, the sun's radiant beams appear, attempting to eradicate the cryptic low-level vapor cloud in the valley below.

The coffee awakes my senses as the flavor-dense bacon dances on my tongue creating a drug-like euphoria. Before long a family in an SUV pulls up behind me to share the view, their windshield in line with the rear of my van. Suddenly, a pickup truck pulls in directly ahead of me, in a way trapping me in. That's when it hits me.

The coffee seems to activate more than just my senses. How far to the next gas station? I have no idea where I am. I neglected my morning ritual and now I added coffee to my system: like tossing gas on a fire, the combination creates panic in my otherwise steadfast demeanor. Frantically, I attempt to reason with myself, but there's no such thing as logic when it comes to emergency bowel movements. What choice is there?

Oh God, there are no trees within a two-minute run of here and I wouldn't make it if there was! I'm done for! Do I do my animalistic business in front of that poor family? That isn't the sight they pulled over to see.

Climbing back in the van and slamming the doors behind me, I do what any responsible soon-to-be-thirty-two-year-old would do, I shit in a plastic Walmart bag, wipe my ass with a road map of Saskatchewan and proceed on my way.

It isn't much longer until I cross into South Dakota, a fact that isn't likely to excite too many people not originating from there. For me, however, today marks a momentous event. I'll finally reach my goal to drink a beer in every state in the country. But, where?

Traditionally, I haven't put much thought into the location, but this one is special, fifty of fifty. I consider the options. Perhaps hike a six-pack to the top of Washington's head on Mount Rushmore? Maybe a roadie on Needles Highway? I call one of the more seasoned beer drinkers I know for advice. His answer comes in the form of an all-knowing scoff, as if no thought should have ever been given to the question at hand. "Sturgis," my dad replies, bluntly.

Fair enough. A biker bar in the iconic town will be a fitting conclusion to the near decade long quest.

Despite my attempts to engage the rather Amazonian blonde bartender at the biker brewery I choose, my special moment is quite anticlimactic. As they often do, one beer flows seamlessly to another until the two pieces of bacon in my otherwise-empty stomach are overwhelmed by the chemical effects of EtOh in the splendid frothy and all-together piquant IPA replacing my lunch. Standing in search of the men's room I notice quickly I've gone from sober to piss drunk at an almost impossibly accelerated rate. No way I can drive right now!

I've been at this fork in the road before. Sit back down and commence with one of my more favorable pastimes, day drinking, or pay the tab and move along? I choose the later of the two on the sole basis that there doesn't seem to be a single person in the establishment willing to entertain me in conversation. Rather than continuing my drive, I find myself posted up in a McDonald's, a block from the brewery, trying to caffeinate away my hard buzz at two in the afternoon, while talking to a man claiming to be the inventor of the things at the end of shoelaces. *It's Tuesday*, I think.

Once more, the road calls me south and I head for the wall of dead presidents. Just north of the monument, however, I feel a halting draw to the tourist trap town of Keystone. A marquee sign advertising rooms for $50 a night is too tempting to pass up. I haven't showered since leaving Hawaii and after wetting my beak in Sturgis, my intention inadvertently redirects from indulging in nature to indulging in malt and hops.

A long shower and change of clothes later, I stroll down the Old West era plank-board sidewalks; cleverly recreated to draw more people to the overpriced stores. A true western saloon with swinging wooden, cowboy doors peaks my interest. I enter with authority, expecting to see a group of misfit cowboys bellied up to the bar with six-shooters hanging from their hips. Old Winchester rifles adorn the walls maintaining the ambiance.

I order a burger as the cover band sets up for their evening set. Sitting among a dozen or so people I sip my drink and can't help but feel completely disconnected from every other person in the room. I feel more alone around people than in the vast, unpopulated mountains of Alaska or the endless, empty beaches of Australia.

Traveling this entire time connected me with so many individual people, but somehow disconnected me from humanity. I'm here and wish to be present, yet have an overwhelming desire to continue this course-less, unrelenting migration. I don't even know how to synthesize and convey what I've absorbed in the past few months. Over two-dozen countries on five continents and now, for some reason, I'm here. A dusty bar, all alone in a crowded room.

Desperate for conversation I order a round for the bar in hopes someone will engage and wish to speak with me. Twelve cheap drinks later and no takers. The place is a tourist trap and as a result, full of tourists. Sans maybe one or two locals, everyone around me is draped in cheesy, overpriced novelty attire showcasing their love for (enter tourist location here).

Scanning the room I attempt to find any commonality. I'm the youngest person here by two and a half decades at least. My hopes to find an interesting human among this lot is about as good as my chances of rappelling off Lincoln's nose tomorrow without being arrested. The whiskey in my glass does what I know it will, gradually shifting manic my mind, bringing me higher.

The next morning the compound effect of those dozen straight whisky drinks wakes me up. South. Still more south. Mount Rushmore presents itself as an impressive human feat from a distance. I'm unwilling to pay the park entrance fee to engage in an elbow war with hordes of frothing tourists looking to capture the same photo taken countless times by countless other busloads of eager sightseers. Instead, I drive ten minutes past the monument and find a large rock formation a short walk from the road, and pull over.

Retrieving my climbing shoes and bag of chalk, I decide to make my own personal connection with the Black Forest stone face and begin to climb until the top of the tallest tree is beneath my feet. Higher. Higher, I climb. Stimulating my childlike bliss. A renewed sense of personal freedom and connection to nature returns to me. I run my fingers through the sun's brilliant warmth. Rejuvenated and triumphant, I once again believe nothing can hold me back, that I and I alone am the narrator of my life's story, the melting point of wax means nothing to me. Until I realize, I'm really high up, and I don't have a way to get down. ❁

About the Author

Leo Jenkins is the popular author of *Lest We Forget: An Army Ranger Medic's Story* and *On Assimilation: A Ranger's Return Home from War*, as well as a contributing writer to *Violence of Action: The Untold Stories of the 75th Ranger Regiment in the War on Terror*, and *Ranger Knowledge: The All-Inclusive Study Guide for Rangers (SOFREP)*.

Jenkins served multiple combat deployments as a special operations medic in the 75th Ranger Regiment during the height of the Global War on Terrorism (GWOT). He's traveled through over three-dozen countries, consumed a beer in all fifty states and continues to seek the road less traveled.

Connect with Leo on:

Facebook: www.facebook.com/leojenkinsauthor

Instagram: www.instagram.com/leo_jenkins

Meet Leo

If you enjoyed reading this book, then you'll enjoy traveling alongside Leo and Marty in the award-winning film, *Nomadic Veterans*.

Nomadic Veterans

Two former Army Rangers, two backpacks, one hundred dollars and three weeks to travel as far around the world as possible. With no plan for travel, Marty Skovlund and Leo Jenkins hop coal trains, hitch rides, and take international flights on a 21-day race against themselves in order to raise money and awareness for the veteran non-profit the GallantFew. Relying on nothing but their veteran network and the good will of strangers, how far will they get?

Winner of the GI Film Festival Founder's Choice Award

Starring: Marty Skovlund, Leo Jenkins

Available on Amazon Video

Appendix 1: Recommended Resources

"The future is meant for those who are willing to let go
of the worst parts of the past."—Corey Taylor

Check out the organizations below, who also offer referrals to other organizations that address the total picture of the interconnected issues you may face.

Are you close to that final act of desperation?

❋ GallantFew: www.gallantfew.org

GallantFew, Inc. coaches, mentors and networks veterans to help them transition to civilian lives filled with hope and purpose. Founded by veterans to veterans, GallantFew's mission is to prevent veteran isolation by connecting new veterans with hometown veteran mentors, thereby facilitating a peaceful, successful transition from military service to a civilian life.

GallantFew does this by creating and supporting a nationwide network of successfully transitioned veterans who engage locally with new veterans with the same military background going through transition. To welcome, connect, and include new veterans, GallantFew motivates communities all over the nation to take responsibility for returning veterans. GallantFew believes this will prevent veteran unemployment, homelessness and suicide.

If you need help, make the call. PLEASE DO NOT TAKE ACTION OF ANY SORT until you talk to:
Phone: Army veteran Karl Monger at 817-600-0514

Phone: Army veteran Clarence Matthews at 843-697-0739
Log online to email GallantFew: www.gallantfew.org/contact/
Facebook: www.facebook.com/gallantfew
Twitter: www.twitter.com/gallantfew
YouTube: www.youtube.com/user/GallantFewInc
Address: P.O. Box 1157, Roanoke, TX 76262

Have the overshadowing cries of your demons silenced you?

❀ Vets4Warriors: www.vets4warriors.com

Vets4WArriors provides 24/7 confidential, stigma-free peer support by veterans to active duty, National Guard and reserve service members, veterans, retirees, and their families and caregivers. All calls are confidential. No information is shared with military branches or units. You are never alone, a caring, empathic veteran or service member is ready to connect with you and follow up.

Vets4WArriors are available to service members and their families who do not want to engage in mental health counseling, as well as, those who currently receive counseling, but need additional support.

Phone: 855-838-8255 Toll Free, available 24 hours a day, 7 days a week for all service members in the U.S.
If serving outside the United States: Call the Global DSN Operator at: DSN 312-560-1110 (Be sure to dial as a DSN number only) or Commercial: 719-567-1110.
Email: Info@Vets4Warriors.com
Log online and chat: www.vets4warriors.com/about/contact.html
Facebook: https://www.facebook.com/Vets4Warriors

Have you slipped into one of the toughest places to get out of—the mind?

❋ Team Red White and Blue

Team Red White and Blue creates quality relationships and experiences that contribute to life satisfaction and overall wellbeing that consists of three core components—health, people, and purpose—which define a rich life.

Team Red White and Blue Team RWB members share more than just values. Team Red White and Blue shares an ethos—a set of guiding beliefs and ideals that characterize our community.

Passion: We care more, we work harder, and we share our story.

People: Veterans and community drive everything we do.

Positivity: We don't ignore the challenges, we just stay positive and attack them.

Commitment: We are dedicated to each other, our mission, and our communities.

Camaraderie: We improve lives through genuine, personal relationships.

Community: This is what we are building…at every level.

Log online to email Team Red White and Blue: www.teamrwb.org/contact-us

Check out a chapter near you: www.teamrwb.org/get-involved/join-the-team

Facebook: www.facebook.com/TeamRWB

Twitter: www.twitter.com/teamrwb

Flickr: www.flickr.com/photos/teamrwb/sets

YouTube: www.youtube.com/user/TeamRWB

Address: 1110 W. Platt St., Tampa, FL 33606

Are you waiting for your next mission to be called a go?

❖ Team Rubicon: www.teamrubiconusa.org

Team Rubicon unites the skills and experiences of military veterans with first responders to rapidly deploy emergency response teams. Team Rubicon's primary mission provides disaster relief to those affected by natural disasters, be it domestic or international. By pairing the skills and experiences of military veterans with first responders, medical professionals, and technology solutions, Team Rubicon aims to provide the greatest service and impact possible.

Through continued service, Team Rubicon seeks to provide our veterans with three things they lose after leaving the military: a purpose, gained through disaster relief; community, built by serving with others; and self-worth, from recognizing the impact one individual can make.

Coupled with leadership development and other opportunities, Team Rubicon looks to help veterans transition from military to civilian life. The driving force behind all of Team Rubicon's operational activity is service above self. Our actions are characterized by the constant pursuit to prevent or alleviate human suffering and to restore human dignity—we help people on their worst days.

Log online to email Team Rubicon: www.teamrubiconusa.org/contact-us

Phone: 310-640-8787

Facebook: www.facebook.com/teamrubicon

Twitter: www.twitter.com/teamrubicon

Instagram: www.instagram.com/teamrubicon

Vimeo: www.vimeo.com/channels/teamrubicon

YouTube: www.youtube.com/user/teamrubiconusa

Google+: www.plus.google.com/+TeamrubiconusaOrg/posts

Address: National Headquarters, 6171 Century Blvd. Suite 310, Los Angeles, CA 90045

Are you struggling with the mental commotion
that occupies your mind?

❋ The Tragedy Assistance Program for Survivors: www.taps.org

The Tragedy Assistance Program for Survivors (TAPS) offers compassionate care to all those grieving the death of a loved one who served in our Armed Forces. Since 1994, TAPS has provided comfort and hope 24 hours a day, seven days a week through a national peer support network and connection to grief resources, all at no cost to surviving families and loved ones. TAPS has assisted over 50,000 surviving family members, casualty officers, and caregivers.

TAPS serves ALL survivors: adult children, children, ex-spouses, extended family, friends and battle buddies, grandparents, parents, siblings, widows/widowers/widowed and significant others through survivor grief seminars, suicide survivor grief seminars, retreats, expeditions, 'inner warrior' events and an online community.

The TAPS Military and Veteran Caregiver Network provides pre- and post-9/11 era military and veteran caregivers with peer support and partners to reduce their isolation and increase their sense of connectedness, engagement, hopefulness, wellness and their knowledge and skills.

800 Phone Number: If you just need someone to talk to, please call TAPS any time at 1.800.959.TAPS (8277). The TAPS survivor care team can also tell you about services and programs you might find helpful. The TAPS resource and information helpline is available 24 hours a day, 7 days a week, 365 days a year.

Phone: 202-588-TAPS (8277) **FAX:** 571-385-2524

Facebook: www.facebook.com/TAPS4America

Twitter: www.twitter.com/TAPS4America

YouTube: www.youtube.com/supporttaps

Address: National Headquarters. 3033 Wilson Boulevard, Suite 630, Arlington, VA 22201

*Have you spent too many nights searching for comfort
at the bottom of a bottle?*

❋ Transformations Treatment Center:
www.transformationstreatment.center

Transformations Treatment Center (TTC) is a primary substance abuse treatment center in Delray Beach, FL. Licensed and accredited by CARF and the Joint Commissions, TTC provides a continuum of care to include: inpatient detox, partial hospitalization, intensive inpatient and outpatient services. Depending upon the client's needs, TTC offers 12-step traditional and Christian dual diagnosis treatment programs lasting between 30 to 90 days. There are four treatment niches: adult, young adult, Christian and first responder/veteran.

TTC takes a holistic approach that not only treats the addiction, but also heals the mind, body and spirit—as well as the family, an important element often overlooked by other treatment centers. TTC offers excellent diagnostics, assessments, treatment planning and medical care to teach all clients how to maintain a lifestyle of recovery worth protecting to get their lives and relationships back on track. TTC takes most insurances. Anyone with Tri-Care can call the admissions number and TTC can refer you to a facility they trust.

Admissions Phone: 877-995-0944

Cell Phone: 561-628-4871

Fax: 561-819-0631

Email Contact: Admissions@transformationstreatment.com

Address: 14000 South Military Trail, Suite 202, Delray Beach Florida, 33484

Facebook: www.facebook.com/TransformationsTC

Twitter: www.twitter.com/ttcrecovery

Instagram: www.instagram.com/ttcrecovery

GallantFew's Recommended Reading List

The Other Side of Me: Memoirs of a Vietnam Marine, Jim Bob Swafford

The Inside Out Revolution, Michael Neill

Man's Search for Meaning, Viktor Frankl

Jesus Was an Airborne Ranger, John McDougall

A Warrior's Garden, Ralph Gaskin

Violence of Action, Marty Skovlund

Lest We Forget, Leo Jenkins

On Assimilation: A Ranger's Return From War, Leo Jenkins

Boots to Loafers: Finding Your New True North, LTC John W Phillips

Other Books
by Leo Jenkins

❀ On Assimilation: A Ranger's Return from War

Some wars don't end, some scars don't heal and some bonds can't be broken. Former U.S. Army Ranger Medic, Leo Jenkins, picks up where he left off with his best-selling book, *Lest We Forget,* to explore the tribulations associated with attempting to reintegrate into society after years at war. Considered one of the most significant introspectives on veteran transition issues ever written, Jenkins lays it all on the line one more time in his book *On Assimilation.*

Foreword: Marty Skovlund, Jr.

Available in both paperback and e-book.

Connect with Leo on:

Facebook: www.facebook.com/leojenkinsauthor

Instagram: www.instagram.com/leo_jenkins

❀ Lest We Forget: An Army Ranger Medic's Story

A rare look inside the life of an Army Ranger medic. The compelling true story of what it takes to become and operate as a special operations medic during the height of the Global War on Terrorism (GWOT). Detailed accounts and pictures from the search and rescue operation for the U.S. Navy Seals who were compromised in the mountains of Afghanistan during Operation Red Wings.

Take a look inside the U.S. special operations medical course as the author trains for the reality of combat in Iraq and Afghanistan. *Lest We Forget* reveals the reality of war and its impact on the individuals who fought for their brothers on their left and right.

Available in both paperback and e-book.

Other Books from Blackside Publishing

❂ The Ghosts of Babylon

War takes from us innocence and delivers an unparalleled view of the world in which we drift. Jonathan Baxter's poetic accounts of war define us, rape us, build us into pillars, and deplete the compassion hiding within our marrow.

For those who've lived it, truly and completely lived it—war is reality. All else a shade of grey in blinding Technicolor. Nothing tastes the way fruit tastes after battle. Following an evening you knew you would not survive, nothing smells as good as the desert rain disrupting the parched arid landscape as the sun rises over the Euphrates.

The warrior poet, an endangered species, should be revered. No academic, regardless how seasoned, will ever convey the essence of war better. No scholar has the capacity to duplicate the nuances splattered in bright red upon these pages: Poignant history told in fluid motion.

The Ghosts of Babylon reflects the emotional and psychological effects of military service, war zone deployments, military separation and assimilation into civilian society. This poetry anthology is based Jonathan Baxter's experiences in Iraq and Afghanistan, first as a U.S. Army Ranger, and later as a private security contractor. Jonathan started writing these poems after his third deployment and continued writing over the course of six years and nine more military and civilian deployments.

Author: Jonathan Baxter
Foreword: Leo Jenkins
Published: August, 2016
Available in both paperback and e-book.

❁ A Soldier to Santiago: Finding Peace on the Warrior Path

Slipping away from reality, a stranger in the civilian world, Brad's military service ended. Could a new veteran like Brad even hope to find peace after witnessing the darkness and the depravity of humanity in war? In *A Soldier to Santiago*, Brad Genereux shares his journey of gradual transformation—from a war-hardened soldier to a man open to the hope of giving and receiving love and acceptance.

Echoing the experiences of other military veterans, Genereux offers a candid account of his struggle to carry out his mission while operating within a convoluted chain of command. Brad's intense journey juxtaposes between a combat zone in Afghanistan and the healing energy of The Way of Saint James.

Is beauty, love, generosity, innocence and forgiveness within grasp of those who've spent their lives and careers pursuing the next mission on behalf of their country? Beyond the veteran audience, this book represents an originative military voice in the realm of the greater Camino literature. Brad hopes readers will ask, "What if transformation *is possible* by undertaking a pilgrimage journey?"

As a career military man, Brad Genereux deployed eleven times around the globe. Deployment demons pursued him until Brad confronted the inner darkness stalking his days and nights while walking the Camino de Santiago, a 500-mile pilgrimage in northern Spain.

Every Spring and Fall, Brad leads other veterans on the Spanish path to peace.

Author: Brad Genereux

Foreword: Heather A. Warfield, Ph.D.

Published: August, 2016

Available in both paperback and e-book.

If you're interested in trekking the Santiago de Camino, contact Brad.

Email: bgenereux@mail.com

Facebook: www.facebook.com/brad.gener.1

❀ Triumph Over Terror

The day that changed the world—September 11, 2001—propelled America into the Global World on Terror (GWOT). Like many Americans who signed up to serve our country, Bob Ossler dropped everything, donned his firefighter turn-out gear, boarded a plane, made his way to Manhattan and joined a long line of people a few blocks from the chaotic confusion of Ground Zero to volunteer and help in any way possible. Escorted to the still smoldering, quaking heap, dubbed "The Pile," Ossler entered into the Gates of Hell—the crematorium and morgue for nearly 3000 beloved souls. Searching for comfort amidst the turmoil, *Triumph Over Terror* explores "Where was God?" in the rubble.

As a professional doing his job, Ossler served on five tours of duty in the weeks and months following 9/11. Bob narrates invaluable eyewitness vignettes recounting the fears, struggles and sacrifices of the Ground Zero workers. Chaplain Ossler honored the bodies and fragmentary remains carried out of the pit and attended to the mourners, the frightened, the wounded, and the heartbroken laborers sifting through millions of tons of carnage for the remains of the unknown, their friends and their faith.

From the broken fragments of men, glass and steel, Ossler weaves a mosaic of God's mercy and grace extended to the desperate overwhelmed by monumental physical, moral and spiritual battles. He chronicles the profound outpourings of heartfelt generosity and heroism from strangers and Americans who just wanted to do "something." Speaking candidly about his questions, fears, exhaustion, stress, and loss of time with his family, Ossler proclaims the courageous and tireless responses from the best of humankind.

Like so many American adults, that barbaric attack etched the trauma of terror deeply into their memories. Yet, a new generation holds no emotional ties to that day of infamy. On the fifteenth anniversary, Ground Zero Chaplain Bob Ossler's firsthand account reminds all Americans to "never forget to honor" the bravery and ultimate sacrifice of first responders who rushed toward terror in hopes of saving civilian lives. Ministering comfort, compassion and a listening ear in the name of God, this book reveals the message of triumph over terror's reign.

Authors: Ground Zero Chaplain Bob Ossler with Janice Kroelinger Hall Heck

Foreword: Tim Shoemaker

Published: August, 2016

Available in both paperback and e-book.

✦ Violence of Action: The Untold Stories of the 75th Ranger Regiment in the War on Terror

Violence of Action is much more than the true, first-person accounts of the 75th Ranger Regiment in the Global War on Terrorism (GWOT). Between the pages lay the heartfelt, first-hand accounts from, and about, the men who lived, fought, and died for their country, their Regiment, and each other.

Objective Rhino, Haditha Dam, recovering Jessica Lynch, the hunt for Zarqawi, the recovery of Extortion 17 and everything in between. Told many times in barracks rooms, bar tables, and backyard barbecues, this book reveals the sights, smells, and emotions of everything that happens in war—good or bad.

Whether you served in the military or are a fan of military history or just want to know more about your fellow man in times of war—this is the book for you.

Authors: Marty Skovlund, Jr. with LTC. Charles Faint and Leo Jenkins

Foreword: Mat Best

Published: October, 2014

Available in both hardcover and e-book.